PORTRAITS OF
AMERICAN PRESIDE...
VOLUME

THE
BUSH
PRESIDENCY

TEN INTIMATE
PERSPECTIVES OF
GEORGE BUSH

Edited by

KENNETH W. THOMPSON

Miller Center of Public Affairs
University of Virginia

UNIVERSITY
PRESS OF
AMERICA

Lanham • New York • Oxford

The Miller Center

University of Virginia

Copyright © 1997 by
University Press of America,® Inc.
4720 Boston Way
Lanham, Maryland 20706

12 Hid's Copse Rd.
Cummor Hill, Oxford OX2 9JJ

Copublished by arrangement with
The Miller Center of Public Affairs,
University of Virginia

The views expressed by the author(s) of this publication do not necessarily represent the
opinions of the Miller Center. We hold to Jefferson's dictum that: "Truth is the proper
and sufficient antagonist to error, and has nothing to fear from the conflict, unless by
human interposition, disarmed of her natural weapons, free argument and debate."

The Bush presidency : ten intimate perspectives of George Bush / edited by
Kenneth W. Thompson.
p.   cm. -- (Portraits of American presidents ; v. 10)
1. Bush, George, 1924-. 2. United States--Politics and government--1989-
1993. I. Thompson, Kenneth W. II. Series.
E176.1P83 1982 vol. 10 (E881) 973'.099 s--dc21   96-40394 CIP
(973.928'092)

ISBN: 0-7618-0670-9 (cloth: alk. ppr.)
ISBN: 0-7618-0671-7 (pbk: alk. ppr.)

♾™ The paper used in this publication meets the minimum requirements of
American National Standard for Information Sciences—Permanence of
Paper for Printed Library Materials, ANSI Z39.48–1984.

To

General Brent Scowcroft

Public Servant, Adviser to Presidents, Strategic Thinker

An example for all who would serve their President,

their country, and their friends

CONTENTS

PREFACE vii
    Kenneth W. Thompson

INTRODUCTION ix
    Kenneth W. Thompson

I. LEADERSHIP AND POLICY-MAKING

1.   THE PRESIDENT AS LEADER 3
      C. Boyden Gray

2.   ORGANIZING FOR POLICY-MAKING 23
      Edward J. Derwinski

II. GOVERNANCE AND
THE BUSH PRESIDENCY

3.   ACCOMPLISHMENTS AND SETBACKS 45
      Clayton Yeutter

4.   THE BUDGET PROCESS 69
      Bryce L. Harlow

III. FORMING AN ADMINISTRATION

5. PERSONNEL AND THE SELECTION PROCESS . . 91
    Chase Untermeyer

IV. THE MAKING OF FOREIGN POLICY

6. THE MAKING OF FOREIGN POLICY IN
    THE BUSH ADMINISTRATION 107
    John R. Bolton

7. THE BUSH PRESIDENCY AND
    INTERNATIONAL ECONOMIC ISSUES 127
    David C. Mulford

V. THE INTELLIGENCE PROCESS

8. INTELLIGENCE IN THE REAGAN AND
    BUSH PRESIDENCIES 143
    Robert M. Gates

VI. THE QUESTION OF PRESIDENTIAL DISABILITY

9. THE BUSH PRESIDENCY AND PRESIDENTIAL
    DISABILITY 165
    Burton J. Lee III, M.D.

VII. THE 1992 ELECTION

10. HOW GEORGE BUSH LOST THE PRESIDENTIAL
    ELECTION IN 1992 183
    Betty Glad

PREFACE

A pattern has emerged in the course of organizing Miller Center Forums up to and including the present volume. We have discovered that major authorities on particular presidents have helped attract others to the University of Virginia. By "word-of-mouth" they have encouraged their friends to join our intellectual enterprise in Faulkner House. Their help has been of inestimable value to a fledgling public affairs center. It has enabled us to further presidential studies in general through the contributions of distinguished visitors to the understanding of contemporary presidents.

Partly by accident and partly by design, our guests have turned the spotlight on certain American presidents. They were viewing particular administrations with shared values but different perspectives. They helped us to understand the president they knew best. The product is a portrait, not a photograph; it helps us see the character and spirit of a leader, not the more or less important details a photograph tends to convey. It tells us what was central to a person's life and works, not what was peripheral. The photograph reveals what can be seen with the naked eye. The portrait shows one thing the photograph cannot reveal: the human essence of the person portrayed.

With this volume, we continue a series of Miller Center publications, "Portraits of American Presidents." We are grateful to the University Press of America for making these volumes available to a wide audience. We have embarked on similar inquiries into all of the postwar presidencies beginning with Franklin D. Roosevelt and Harry S. Truman and including Dwight D. Eisenhower, John F. Kennedy, Lyndon Baines Johnson, Richard M. Nixon, Gerald Ford, Jimmy Carter, and Ronald Reagan. The presidency of George Bush will be remembered for blending continuity and change. While

Bush sought to continue many of the policies of Reagan, he also took initiatives that were departures from Reagan, especially in foreign policy. We plan to continue the series with additional volumes on Bush and Bill Clinton. In the introduction that follows, the editor traces the Center's interest in the presidency of George Bush.

INTRODUCTION

Nearly a decade has passed since George Bush sought the presidency of the United States. Few presidents if any have brought the experience and background he offered to the presidency. He had served as vice president for two terms in the Reagan presidency. He had been a member of the House of Representatives and chairman of the Republican party. He held the post of director of Central Intelligence and represented his country in the People's Republic of China. In these and other positions, he had demonstrated a knowledge of government and a capacity to act and make decisions.

Beginning in 1993, we invited some 40 members of the Bush administration to come to Charlottesville for intensive discussions of the president they served. Some were members of the Bush White House. Some had been Cabinet officials. A few were special envoys. We tried to attract others who had been political advisers, press representatives, speech writers, and counsel to the president. As with previous oral histories, we invited journalists who had covered President Bush, scholars who had written about the Bush presidency, and critics as well as friends of the administration.

The group who stand out in our Bush oral history are the outstanding figures who assisted in the development of the Bush foreign policy. They constitute a collection of seasoned and extraordinarily capable officials, most of whom had served in previous administrations. Brent Scowcroft's ability as national security adviser was confirmed by the Miller Center oral history. After the Center's inquiry, who can doubt that he fulfilled as no one before or since the requirements set forth in the National Security Act of 1946. According to the late James Forrestal, who drafted the main provisions for the office, the task of the adviser is "to bundle together" the main strands of foreign policy emanating from the departments and agencies concerned in diverse ways with the subject. The task of the adviser is to supply the president with the advice and substantive information flowing from an administration. The mission of the adviser is not to be the president's spokesman on foreign policy, unless the president wills it. He or she is not generally considered to be a policymaker. While the words are not used in the creation of the office, the NSC adviser, much like the presidential advisers named in the report of the president's committee on administrative management of 1937, should have "a passion for anonymity." Scowcroft had much to do with the cooperative and harmonious spirit that prevailed in President Bush's foreign policy team. Many observers see him as the ideal NSC adviser and the backbone of Bush's foreign policy.

Another member of the Bush foreign policy team who has played a significant role in the Miller Center's oral history is Lawrence S. Eagleburger. Over a long career of nearly four decades in the foreign service, he held most of the important policy-making positions. He capped his public service as secretary of state in the Bush administration. The Miller Center has benefited enormously from his contributions as policymaker in residence. He has also had a hand in the Center's invitations to participants in our oral history.

For any president, the question of leadership is central to judging that president. C. Boyden Gray is uniquely qualified to discuss President Bush as leader. As counsel to the President, he maintained a close watch over a multitude of presidential actions and policies. His portfolio of duties included ethics, judicial appointments, and the powers of the Oval Office. He discusses personnel appointments in the administration and in particular problems of delay. According to General Gray, Bush helped create a strong economy. He passed sweeping civil rights legislation, notably the bill on American disability. Why, then, was he not reelected? One reason was that the nation suffered what Gray defines as a white-collar recession. Press coverage of his campaign was "very nasty." The press drummed the idea of a recession into people's consciousness. Gray dismisses the idea that a change occurred in Bush's health or mental attitude. Gray also answers questions concerning Bush's ability as a speaker, his charisma or lack of it, his speech writers, the 1990 "budget deal" with Congress, and changes in the distribution of power between the executive and the Congress affecting the Bush presidency. He describes and criticizes approaches to the budget process and the tax cut. He offers favorable assessments of Barbara Bush and John Sununu and argues that the death of Lee Atwater unquestionably influenced the outcome of the 1992 election. He concludes by answering questions on Oliver North, Nicaragua, and Clarence Thomas.

Edward J. Derwinski was an early participant in the Bush oral history. He was administrator of the Veterans Administration and then secretary of veterans affairs. Earlier, he was counselor to the Department of State. In 1967 he was a fifth-term congressman when George Bush was a freshman congressman. He recounts Bush's efforts as ambassador to the United Nations and provides a realistic appraisal of the role of the Bush Cabinet and of the White House staff. Bush's relations with Congress are described as "good on the surface but horrible beneath the surface," referring to the Democratic-controlled Congress. He analyzes the rationale of certain Cabinet appointments and discusses President Bush's strengths and weaknesses. Derwinski is critical of the way the campaign was managed. He concludes with a comparison of the "old" and "new" Congress and the bureaucracy.

Part II throws the spotlight on governance and the Bush presidency. The two contributors are both supporters and critics of the administration. Clayton Yeutter was secretary of agriculture in the Bush administration and U.S. trade representative under President Reagan. He had planned to leave government after Reagan's departure, but admiration for George Bush led him to continue. He is critical of Bush because of the breach of "the no new taxes" promise, which turned the conservatives against him, mainly because of press reaction. Yeutter discusses the recession and one of its causes, namely, the credit crunch that affected small businesses and prolonged the recession. Paradoxically, the ending of the Cold War hurt Bush because of the downsizing that occurred and not only in defense industries. Spending discipline declined, notably with entitlements. The Bush record on trade was excellent, especially on NAFTA and the Enterprise for the Americas Initiative. The Bush record on agriculture, education, labor, global warming—and in particular the Global Warming Treaty of the administration—health care, transportation legislation, crime, drugs, and family values is outstanding.

Bryce L. Harlow is one of the younger leaders in the Bush administration who was assistant secretary of the treasury for legislative affairs. He is frank to say that the first two years of the administration defined its future for the entire four-year period. Harlow chronicles the administration's decision to proceed incrementally with budget legislation. That meant a small package in 1989 and a big package in 1990. In 1989, the initiative on the small package was linked with a reduction of the capital gains tax. This led to a struggle with the Democratic leadership and the poisoning of the atmosphere for future cooperation. When the negotiating groups were reduced in size in 1990, it led to further problems, arising in part from holding negotiations in the Oval Office, and to premature involvement by President Bush. A second mistake was the administration's failure to keep Republicans informed and reassured of their actions. When the announcement was made about including new revenues, some Republicans felt betrayed, and the Democrats lost interest over the summer. The scene shifted to Andrews Air Force Base in what Harlow called "a decadent experience." The scene of the negotiations changed again, and the negotiating group was reduced, including Newt Gingrich. Republicans felt betrayed. The administration lost Republican votes, but even more seriously, they squandered the sense of trust they had developed. Harlow concludes his presentation by discussing timing in the handling of foreign and domestic policy and the administration's strategy being overcome by the aggression of Saddam Hussein.

Part III of the volume is addressed to the selection of personnel and the forming of an administration. Chase Untermeyer was director of presidential personnel for the Bush administration. He notes that George Bush was the first president since FDR who had known every member of his Cabinet before appointing them to office. He draws a clear distinction between Cabinet and staff. Untermeyer does point to one exception. C. Boyden Gray was involved in policy-making when he was counsel to the President in the White House. Untermeyer considers that he should have devoted himself entirely to being the President's lawyer. Untermeyer speaks favorably of John Sununu. He also praises Bush's ability to deal with crises. Untermeyer describes in some detail his own responsibilities and how he handled them. He discusses the campaign of 1992 and rejects the thesis that the result was in any way connected with Bush's health. Rather, he insists that Bush had been successful in calling the shots in past campaigns. The President believed he could come from behind as he had many times before. Untermeyer points to the death of three men: Lee Atwater, Malcolm Baldridge, and Dean Burch. If they had lived, the results might have been different. Cabinet-level people, including the deputy secretary of state, are selected by the president himself. The discussion concludes with a comparison of how prominent sub-Cabinet appointments are made in some administrations and how they were made in the Bush administration.

Part IV contains chapters on foreign policy and international economic issues. John R. Bolton was assistant secretary of state for international organization affairs in the Bush administration. He played a significant role in coordinating relations with the United Nations in the Gulf War. His association with James Baker went back to 1978. Bolton attributes his appointment to Baker. He compares previous intraparty transitions with the Bush transition. Bush centralized personnel appointments in the White House rather than delegating appointments to Cabinet secretaries. Everyone noted the close relationship of the President and Baker. Bolton compares it with the relationship between President Kennedy and his brother Bobby. Decisions on key issues were often made through the use of cameras and television screens, saving the time of going to the White House.

The Congress played a relative insignificant role on the Gulf War until the end of the process. When Saddam invaded Kuwait, Congress was in its August recess and most congressmen were just as happy because of the uncertainties of Gulf policies. Congress remained on the sidelines until November and during the decision by the administration and the United Nations to use force. Indeed, it remained on the margins of decision making throughout the U.N. authorization. Bolton recounts the manner in which Congress became engaged in the decision to use force. Bolton was also heavily involved in the U.N. decision through studying past Security Council decisions on matters of this kind. He gives specific examples that demonstrate the extent to which Bush was truly "a hands-on president." He goes on to review the Somalia action and the weighing of the options that led to U.S. intervention. He writes in conclusion about decision making in Somalia, Bush's personal diplomacy, Bush's style in building an alliance, the transformation of the initiatives for diplomats on the ground, retiring Security Council resolutions as against allowing them a long life, Thatcher and Bush, the main reason for Bush's defeat, diplomacy leading up to the vote on the Gulf War, and country votes in the United Nations.

The second chapter in Part IV is by David C. Mulford, who was undersecretary and assistant secretary of international affairs in the Treasury Department. Today he is chairman of CS First Boston Europe. He was a senior policy official in Treasury from 1984, serving under Regan, Baker, and Brady. Mulford considers the handling of international economic issues a lasting accomplishment of the Bush administration. He focuses especially on the Bush approach to the problem of international indebtedness of the major countries of Latin America. The problem came to light in 1982 when Mexico defaulted on its debt—followed by Brazil and other Latin American countries, with the exception of Colombia. U.S. banks accounted for 32 percent of the total of the loans. Some feared the threat of a Great Depression in the United States if the debts were not handled effectively. Mulford describes the initiatives that were taken, including the Baker (James) Plan, under which great syndicates of 400 to 500 banks would make new money available under "forced" lending operations. They would provide new credit and roll over existing debts. The IMF would help countries initiate programs to reform their economies. The Baker Plan was unsuccessful, and rescheduled debts continued to grow relentlessly. The countries were falling into deeper recession with higher unemployment and high inflation. When Bush was elected in November 1988, the so-called Latin American debt problem, which included Poland and Central Europe, occupied his and Secretary Brady's attention. The debt had to be reduced—that is, forgiven.

Mulford tells the story of how the problem was addressed. If third world debts were forgiven, what about equivalent actions for debtors in the United States? The Brady Plan provided an answer, and the countries of Latin America broke the cycle of revolutionary collapse and revolution. Bush followed the Brady Plan with the Enterprise Initiative for the Americas whose goal was to stimulate investment and trade without neglecting the debt problems of the smaller countries. The Bush administration negotiated the North American Free Trade Agreement, which came into effect in the first year of the Clinton presidency. President Bush proposed a similar approach for Poland to the Group of Seven (G-7). Since then, Poland's economy has grown at a rate of up to 9 percent per year. Finally, the administration led the way toward facilitating Russian economic adjustment even before the fall of the Berlin Wall.

Parts V, VI, and VII encompass intelligence, presidential disability, and the 1992 elections in the Bush administration. Single-authored chapters are addressed to each topic in turn. Robert Gates was director of Central Intelligence from 1991 to 1993. Dr. Burton J. Lee III was physician to President Bush from 1989 to 1993. Professor Betty Glad of the Department of Government and International Affairs at the University of South Carolina is president of the International Society for Political Psychology.

Robert Gates served under four presidents in the White House and six at CIA. He emphasizes the continuity of policy from president to president. More and more, intelligence archives are opening up, and scholars are gaining access to National Intelligence Estimates. Gates argues that whereas the public has focused on covert action and large estimates of the future, neither compares to the daily "river of information" that flows into the policy community from the field. President Bush had a better perception than any of his predecessors on what intelligence can and cannot do. Others have tended to overestimate or underestimate its role.

President Bush also demonstrated skill in managing relations with the former Soviet Union. He kept NATO intact, continued arms control efforts, and facilitated domestic reforms and the gradual relaxing of Soviet dominance over East Europe. Gates dismisses the criticism that Bush stayed with Gorbachev too long. A country can have only one president at a time. Gates discusses whether the administration misread Saddam Hussein's intentions. No one had any illusions, but there was evidence that he would need more time to prepare for war. The Shi'a and Kurdish uprisings after the Iraq War appeared less likely to some forecasters than a military uprising. Gates also responds to questions about events before and since the Bush presidency.

Dr. Lee was both a friend of the Bush family and presidential physician to President Bush. He is a distinguished authority on cancer, having been a leading scientist at the Sloan-Kettering Cancer Center and a member of various presidential commissions. He was involved in the Miller Center's inquiry into presidential disability and the 25th Amendment. He played an important role in organizing the White House plan to deal with any instance of presidential disability. He dealt with President Bush's fibrillation and his thyroid episode. In his chapter, Dr. Lee discusses their experience with Grave's disease. With this and other medical problems, Lee saw to it that the Bushes had the benefit of top medical consultants. President Bush's illness in Tokyo was minor, and Dr. Lee gives a full account of the episode. Should civilian physicians or military doctors be the presidential physician? Dr. Lee explores the question. Should he be a friend of the president? In some ways, yes, because the physician must have the president's trust. Dr. Lee goes on to assess the job and conditions for effectiveness. The picture as he describes it is not encouraging, and yet he had significant accomplishments. Dr. Lee also examines the crucial role of the vice president in determining disability. No presidential physician was more highly motivated to understand his role than Dr. Lee.

Finally, Professor Betty Glad, a well-respected political scientist, reviews the 1992 election. As president of the International Society for Political Psychology, she weighs the possibility that Bush's patrician background may have been a factor. She questions his version of the Oval Office strategy in 1992—stay at home as long as possible and appear presidential. Glad lists five structural factors that may account for the President's defeat. She assesses the distrust that conservatives in the Republican party felt for him. She gives evidence of Bush's strategy of negative campaigning not working. He made ideological, tactical, and stylistic errors. She undertakes to explain the basis of his complacency. He failed to address the concerns and feelings of people. His rhetoric had an eccentric quality that did not match the man. When all is said and done, he might have won if Perot had not re-entered the presidential campaign. In Panama and the Gulf War, Bush demonstrated resolve and courage. As for the various psychological theories that would account for his defeat, Americans are deeply divided as to psychological interpretations and psychohistory. In the end, we are left with the all important and as yet unanswered question, "Why did George Bush lose the 1992 presidential election?"

I

LEADERSHIP
AND POLICY-MAKING

CHAPTER 1

THE PRESIDENT AS LEADER*

C. BOYDEN GRAY

NARRATOR: We are delighted that C. Boyden Gray could be with us to share his thoughts on the Bush administration. Mr. Gray was born in Winston-Salem, North Carolina. He graduated *magna cum laude* from Harvard with a degree in history. He was first in his class and editor in chief of the Law Review at the University of North Carolina Law School. He clerked for Chief Justice Earl Warren and after his clerkship joined the Washington law firm of Wilmer, Cutler and Pickering, where he soon became a partner.

In 1981 Mr. Gray was named legal counsel to Vice President Bush in the Reagan administration and in 1985, counsel. He was also counsel to the Presidential Task Force on Regulatory Relief, which then-Vice President Bush chaired. In 1988 he became director of the Office of Transition Counsel for the Bush team, and in January 1989 he was named counsel to President George Bush. At the end of the Bush administration, he returned to Wilmer, Cutler and Pickering, where he specializes in advice on regulatory matters, especially as they relate to the environment. He is a member of the Harvard Committee on University Development as well as several other committees. Mr. Gray is chairman of the board of St. Mark's School and a recipient of the Presidential Citizens' Medal.

Presented in a Forum at the Miller Center of Public Affairs on 17 February 1994.

MR. GRAY: My job at the White House involved ethics, judicial appointments, and the powers of the Oval Office. It offered a unique opportunity for me to see how the government works or, depending upon one's point of view, doesn't work. I had a rather unique, extraordinary opportunity for which I am very grateful, but which I probably would never do again.

With regard to the current ethics wars in the Clinton administration, I am very sympathetic to the problems that President Clinton has had. The appointment process under George Bush was also slow, as the paperwork and hurdles are quite steep. One has to go through this form, that form, this form—the process keeps repeating itself. Congress has made it absolutely imperative that the definitions and approaches taken to fill out one's tax form are *not* to have any relevance to how one fills out a financial disclosure form. In the job I had, one's time is spent filling out and then reviewing forms.

President Bush evinced some frustration with this endless process, and I knew he was going to go after me in the first and only staff meeting that he attended in its entirety in February 1989. I could tell that he was just going through the motions as he talked to people around the table. Finally he got to me and said, "Boyd, how come we can't get so-and-so cleared? He has been through this before. In the Reagan administration he was confirmed as ambassador to country *X*, where he now is. What is the problem?" With an inward sigh of relief because he had picked the only individual for whom I had a legitimate excuse, I replied, "Mr. President, he hasn't filed any income tax returns since he left the United States." "Well," the President said as he slapped his thigh, "I guess I had better pick a better example next time."

One of the big puzzles to me is how someone who, I will argue, had such a strong legacy could lose the election. To his successor, Bush left a very strong policy in terms of U.S. military posture, which is an obligation of any president to do. North Korea is now emerging as a severe problem, but otherwise, what President Clinton inherited with respect to the fundamental interest of the United States was a strong set of cards to play, especially if one includes President Clinton's own success in getting the NAFTA agreement passed in Congress. The country is on very solid foreign policy footing.

As for domestic policy, President Bush often took the view that the first major rule was to do no harm; do not mess things up, which governments have a tendency to do. Not only did he not create problems, he left a very strong economy—very low inflation, very low interest rates, declining deficit, very high productivity that is critical to maintaining low inflation and international competitiveness, and a relatively manageable regulatory burden, which is an important, but often difficult to explain, part of the economic picture. This picture is much different from the one Reagan inherited in 1981. We have, for example, the best urban air quality of any country in the world, and yet we managed to achieve that goal without sacrificing economic productivity.

Bush was also responsible for what was understood at the time to be the most sweeping civil rights legislation in 25 years—the American Disability Act. He broke the back of the quota approach that I think has done so much harm in a political correctness sense to the basic premise of our nation, which is supposed to be a melting pot. He took many hits for that move, but he had a great deal of courage and saw it through to the end.

One of his big failures was his inability to sustain the veto of the cable bill. If you think that is a small detail, think about the struggle potential producers of television programs are having concerning who will be granted the rights to produce these programs. Will it be anyone who has an idea and can produce it, or will it be just the three major networks that we have had for so long?

In short, he left a very strong economy. A big debate is now taking place about how much credit President Clinton can take for the economy, but it doesn't really matter to President Clinton whether he produced it or not. He certainly is getting the benefit of it, and that situation cannot be altered.

In view of these strong points, why wasn't George Bush reelected? I believe that the economy and the perception of the economy are the responsible factors. We had a very vicious recession—vicious in the sense that it was for the first time a white-collar recession and not a blue-collar recession where workers get laid off but with a high likelihood of being rehired. Blue-collar recessions are common occurrences; they have happened cyclically many times over the years. People in this white-collar recession who had lost their desk jobs or office jobs knew that they were very unlikely to be rehired. The parents of students in college and graduate school were watching with horror as their sons and daughters were simply not getting hired into comfortable white-collar careers.

The white-collar recession, in turn, was a result of the financial crisis of the banks, savings and loans institutions, and insurance. This combination made for a very ugly recession. Among those hit as a result were the media. Most aspects of the media, except cable television (which may explain why it got hammered politically), suffered huge losses. If an industry is able to escape losses in the marketplace, sometimes it gets hammered politically. In any case, the media may have been disposed to treat President Bush more harshly than they might otherwise have treated a candidate for reelection because of the type of recession.

Whatever the cause of the coverage, it was very nasty. Someone quantified the figures and discovered that the number of stories about the recession were tripled. During 1992 the use of the word *recession* was representative of the type of coverage being provided by the media. It appeared an average of three times in every network news broadcast, but the interesting thing is that we were not in a recession in 1992. The recession had ended in 1991. The year 1992, in fact, was a rather handsome year in terms of GDP growth. I remember vividly in the fall when they released the first run of the second quarter GDP figures, pegged at 2.8 percent. The media went nuts and said that President Bush had been manipulating the data from the Commerce Department. They reported that the growth was not 2.8 percent, because as we all knew, this year was the worst since the Great Depression. When the final figures came out after the election, it wasn't 2.8 percent; it was 3.6 percent. Growth for the entire year turned out to be 3.9 percent, compared to the first year of the Clinton presidency, which was 2.9 percent. The press, however, has decided that 1992 just doesn't exist. It can't be found in the press coverage.

In early February 1994, the press covered the preliminary figures for 1993. Last quarter, GDP growth equalled 5.9 percent, as compared to Bush's last quarter in which he was defeated that consisted of 5.7 percent growth. The press—including the *New York Times, Wall Street Journal,* and *Washington Post*—said that the entire year of 1993 had 2.9 percent growth as opposed to 1992, which contained 2.6 percent growth. The 2.6 percent figure that they reported, however, is a false one. The Commerce Department had made the figures public in a very confusing way, and the press, either intentionally or unintentionally, regurgitated false data. This report is nevertheless the fulcrum about which this question of the election turned, and we didn't do a good job of dispelling the negative and false perceptions about the economy. In that sense, perhaps we deserved to lose.

To reiterate, I believe the state of the country, the state of the government, and the image of the United States abroad that President Bush left was strong in every respect and will be so understood by historians.

NARRATOR: A few of your predecessors have talked about a change in President Bush. Having known him for 40 years, they have said that George Bush has had a very evident vitality and enthusiasm for all aspects of life. As the election approached, however, he delayed the campaign and his entry into the campaign, and he appeared to have lost some of his nerve. Even in private conversations, they felt he didn't have quite the energy and enthusiasm that he previously had. Your position in the White House makes you well qualified to comment on this issue. What are your observations?

MR. GRAY: I saw him a great deal except when he was on the road campaigning, and during that time and up until the campaign, I never saw the change that you mentioned. I actually played tennis with him two days before he went into the hospital, and for a man in his late 60s, he played extraordinarily well. In fact, he bailed me out! I was astonished.

In terms of his health or mental attitude, I didn't see any change. He had become increasingly bitter about the press over the course of the year and what it had done to his son Neal, who had to declare personal bankruptcy and move out of Denver. That situation was a big weight on his shoulders, and I think he was increasingly disenchanted with the hammering he and his family were getting. He knew that public scrutiny and public criticism came with the territory and didn't complain about it publicly, but he would complain to me privately. His bitterness about the press may have taken some of the fun out of the job for him.

Certainly, I can attest to my own view about public life. People say, "You must miss the excitement," to which I reply, "No,

I got out a half-step ahead of the sheriff, and I am proud of it. If I had spent another six months in government, I would have been indicted." People then ask, "For what?" I answer, "I don't know! Just for being there!" The media was very nasty at the end of President Bush's term, which may explain the change some have noted.

George Bush thought he was going to win. He thought he was going to have a comeback. He is, of course, a world-class athlete, which may explain why he got ready for the campaign late. George Bush makes comebacks. That is the way he plays tennis, baseball, and horseshoes. An article was printed in *Sports Illustrated* about his horseshoe match and about how Bush was trailing all the way to the last throw, when he won the game. That is the way he was, and I think he would have taken Clinton out at the end except for Perot. The horrible Weinberger reindictment didn't help him either. Historians will analyze this factor forever—this ugly little reindictment that just happened to occur the weekend before the election. It was totally unnecessary, totally gratuitous, and it had nothing new to say. The press went crazy over the story, and the result can actually be traced in the tracking polls. The polls show Bush closing in on Clinton and then the whole thing fell apart the Saturday after the reindictment. I think President Bush holds an enormous bitterness about that incident, the full extent of which he probably hasn't even shared with me.

QUESTION: Regarding the 1990 Clear Air Amendments, what would you consider the strongest and weakest points of the legislation? Second, given the enormous number of possible actors—the EPA, civil servants, Congress, special interest groups, the White House—who played a role in the passage of those amendments? From your experience, what would you consider to be the White House's most appropriate and important role in formulating environmental legislation?

MR. GRAY: Leaving this kind of legislation to bureaucrats really means abdicating responsibility because the bureaucrats will in turn build their empires, which is what they should do. A GM auto worker will try to make as many cars as he or she can. An EPA environmental rule writer will try to make as many rules as he or she can. The difference, at least in this country, is that if the public doesn't buy the cars, no more can be made. Russia is trying to learn this lesson—if they do not have a military to buy the steel anymore, no one is going to buy it.

Some accountability over the bureaucrats must exist. Many different interests are competing and sometimes converging—such as the EPA, the Department of Energy, and the Federal Energy Regulatory Commission—an independent agency that operates independently of the EPA (although it shouldn't) and regulates natural gas with more impact on natural gas use than even the Natural Gas Regulatory Agency. The only place all of these different agencies and interests can be coordinated is the White House.

As for the best and worst parts—the worst part is the paperwork. To describe the mind-numbing paperwork requirements in the permitting time would put everyone to sleep. We did let that legislation get away from us. I didn't focus on it soon enough myself, and it is now in rather serious litigation over what will actually result. We tried to simplify the impact and the rules that were written to carry out the provisions, but they are now in litigation.

The strongest point of the 1990 amendments was the privatized enforcement of acid rain regulation. This legislation is the biggest single piece of regulation probably ever to be adopted. It sought a 50 percent reduction in sulfur dioxide (SO_2) emissions in the United States, which is a ten-million-ton reduction. This proposal was extraordinarily ambitious and is now being implemented with extraordinary ease and lack of disruption. We measured things in environmental terms by the cost per ton of removal. What does it cost per ton of SO_2, nitrogen oxide, or volatile organic compound (VOC) removal? It was thought that the cost per ton for acid rain would be $1,000 or $1,500 per ton. It turned out that the market mechanism put in place—privatized enforcement allowing utilities to trade emission allowances back and forth—has driven the cost to below $200 a ton. It is an absolutely astonishing vindication of the power of the marketplace. The big question is whether similar mechanisms that are authorized for other parts of the act will be put into place and allowed to flourish in the Clinton administration the way they are now working for acid rain.

QUESTION: Would you make some comments concerning the charismatic qualities of Mr. Bush? He followed a man who was unusually good at communicating with the people and selling them his point of view. During that time, Mr. Bush sat in the background, which is the nature of the office of vice president. His opponent, who is now in office, is yet a different charismatic mix—a so-called born salesman. Given the attitude that Mr. Bush had about the press, did he not have the charismatic quality and the ability to use the force of his office to exercise leadership rather than make complaints?

MR. GRAY: The complaints were made in private. President Bush could be a very good speaker, but he was no Ronald Reagan. Very few people are, will be, or have been as effective as Reagan. Nevertheless, he could be a good speaker, and he pulled some of Reagan's chestnuts out of the fire. I remember vividly the debate with Geraldine Ferraro (I was in charge of the mechanics of it). He was sandwiched in between two Reagan debates on the theory that he would do so badly that President Reagan had to protect him. It turned out that Reagan's first debate was the disaster. He didn't prepare his summation. He got lost on Highway 1 in California and wandered all over the state, if you remember. As a result, Reagan's age became an issue, and the effect of this first debate was reflected in the tracking polls, which showed Reagan's popularity plummeting. All eyes at that point were on Vice President Bush. I knew my career hung in the balance on this debate. I can remember various people staring at me, but Bush did a fabulous job and stabilized the polling. By the time of Reagan's second debate, he was back up in the polls to where he had been before his own first debate.

I can also remember the campaign throughout Europe to persuade the Germans, Belgians, Italians, and the British to allow the installation of the Pershing missiles. Both Helmut Kohl and Margaret Thatcher were in trouble politically. The peace movement was making great headway. Then, Bush went on a whistle-stop tour of Europe and single-handedly turned around and defeated the Soviets' number-one priority during the 1980s. It was an absolutely incredible performance. They installed the Pershings, and that move was the beginning of the end in terms of the Soviet Union, in my opinion. In short, Bush was capable of extraordinary performances.

One of the puzzles to which I do not know the answer is why he seemed not to have the same skills as president that he had as vice president. For example, people were unaware that virtually all of Reagan's speech writers during his second term were recruited from George Bush's vice-presidential staff. In short, the Great Communicator's speech writers in the second term had been recruited and trained by the "Non-Communicator" vice president.

The question, then, might be, if Bush could have such high quality people as vice president, why couldn't he have people of equal ability as president. The speech writers, with all due respect, were not of the same caliber as their predecessors in Bush's office when he was vice president, and their absence did affect his ability to communicate. Incidentally, President Bush has acknowledged in a recent interview that he somehow was not able to communicate effectively.

NARRATOR: Did Bush's remark after the Ferraro debate hurt him politically?

MR. GRAY: I don't think that comment had much impact on the debate. It certainly didn't show up in the tracking polls. Besides, for every person that was offended, there was probably someone saying, "Great!" In short, he may have turned some people off, but he may have also turned some people on with that statement.

What the public wanted to know at that time was whether they could trust Bush should something happen to Reagan. Because Reagan was so old, they wanted to know that he was backed by someone who had real energy and capability, and Bush's performance gave that message loud and clear.

QUESTION: I have always been perplexed by the 1990 budget deal with Congress. Obviously, that deal had devastating political consequences for the Bush presidency, but it did not appear to have any significant impact on reducing the budget. Could you comment on this issue?

MR. GRAY: President Bush said during the campaign and also recently that it was a bad deal. I suppose one should learn that you cannot trust Congress to keep their end of the bargain. After all, they never have, so why should we expect them to do so in the future?

In the larger context, this situation is an example of the public's lack of appreciation for the extraordinary difficulties faced by a chief executive in his interactions with Congress. The deck is stacked heavily against a president. For example, the ethics rules, which were my responsibility, are the modern-day weaponry used by Congress against the president. The weapons have become much more subtle, but they are also more difficult to fight. It didn't used to be this way. I remember a story that I have often heard because of my height (I am 6'6") about my 6'8" ancestor who didn't like dueling. Apparently, this ancestor got into an argument with Stephen Douglas of the Lincoln-Douglas debates. Douglas, who was 5'4" tall, challenged my ancestor to a duel, his choice of both weapon and place. My ancestor agreed and said, "Broad swords in the middle of the Potomac." They waded in approximately two or three feet, and Douglas was under water.

That was the civilized way to resolve a disagreement. Now people go after your reputation, and it is pretty nasty stuff. The thing that the American public doesn't fully appreciate is that the rules apply only to us; Congress has exempted itself from them. They are able to fire these Pershing missiles at you, and you have a BB gun with which to defend yourself. They have exempted themselves from everything. In *The Federalist* No. 57, James Madison defended against critics who said that the House of Representatives was becoming an elite body divorced from the people and that Royalists were becoming an institution. He argued that the biggest reason why this scenario would never happen is that representatives would never dare pass a law and impose it on the public while exempting themselves from it. Well, of course they do that routinely. Madison said that if they ever did do that, it would be the surest sign of a descent into tyranny. I am not suggesting that we are experiencing congressional tyranny, but an uneven playing field does make it difficult for a president to operate.

In the foreign policy arena, Congress took advantage of Watergate by passing the War Powers Resolution, which they thought would cripple the president in his ability to use force. No president, not even a Democratic president, has acknowledged the constitutionality of that resolution. President Bush basically ignored it in the Persian Gulf War. Nothing is said about it now in connection with Bosnia, Somalia, or Haiti.

On the budget side, however, what Congress did was to take away the president's impoundment authority, which had given him the leverage necessary to play in the budget process. Impoundment is very much like a line-item veto. Any of the 43 state governors who have this authority will say that it is impossible to govern without it. The president, on the other hand, doesn't have such authority and therefore has no leverage with the jackals at the other end of Pennsylvania Avenue. It is extremely difficult to deal with a Senator Byrd who has all of the cards and money that is to be allocated. One quarter of the Senate is on his committee, and he plays them like a Stradivarius. It is very difficult for the two branches to connect on the budget front under those circumstances.

Every candidate for the presidency, including Clinton and Perot, has argued for the line-item veto. It is, in my opinion, an essential power for the presidency to regain. If one looks at a chart and sees where the budget deficits begin to occur, it is clear that the revenues have been fairly stable. It is the spending that has gotten out of control, and the increases began in 1974 when the Congressional Budget and Impoundment Control Act was passed, taking away from the president his impoundment authority, a power the president had possessed for 180 years. President Clinton's difficulties will be every bit as severe as President Bush's as a result.

QUESTION: Do you think that the voters and the psychology of elections is returning to a more balanced, less emotional view of the issues? In other words, are we likely to have a more balanced electorate in future elections that is less swayed by emotional oratory?

MR. GRAY: When President Bush lost the election, of course his supporters were greatly disappointed, but I'm not sure that the electorate was unbalanced in any way. I think President Clinton speaks with great passion; however, not everything he says is completely accurate, and I think the public sees through that. I don't think it was oratory that won or lost the 1992 election any more than I think it was oratory on the part of Reagan that won the election in 1981.

I believe that the economy is what mostly determines presidential elections, and the economy was terrible in 1981. Reagan probably won the election as a result. Similarly, the economy was thought to be terrible in 1992, although it wasn't, but that perception is why Clinton won.

QUESTION: You mentioned the veto of a cable bill in your presentation. Would you expand on your comments regarding the bill that was passed and relate the bill to what has been happening in the past weeks with the relationship between the cable companies and the so-called phone companies? It appears that a huge expansion in that area is likely to take place.

MR. GRAY: The cable bill is one of many reasons that some have decided to throw in the towel and marry with the telephone company. He saw the difficulty of financing the information highway by himself, or of cable doing it by itself.

I was totally disqualified from this issue during my White House years because of my family's involvement in the cable industry. Thus, I am biased. I am saying only what I know as a private citizen, not by virtue of any inside information I obtained in the government because I stayed out of the issue completely.

People in the cable industry are quite blunt in saying that the cable bill very much followed the same pattern of other regulatory initiatives under the federal government. That is to say—and this process again is not something the public generally understands— economic regulation almost never occurs solely because some congressman, staff member, or bureaucrat of the EPA or whatever agency decides that it is good to regulate. Regulation, instead, usually happens because a competitor in the marketplace decides they want to use the government to gain an advantage over someone else. In fact, it happens every day. Most regulation is a result of segment A of an industry trying to gain an advantage or eliminate a disadvantage in relation to segment B, C, D, or E. In the case of the cable industry, the networks saw a solid, continuing decline in market share and decided to apply some pressure to the cable companies. They couldn't beat them in the marketplace, so they decided to do it politically. That, perhaps, seems somewhat provocative, but it is the way a regulatory system usually works. The Clean Air Act, for example, has been a three-decade war, not open to the public. The public doesn't see what takes place, that the process is moved by brown envelopes of PAC money going to John Dingell and his colleagues in the House, Senate, and Energy and Commerce committees.

For example, until the Clean Air Act, an atmosphere of total war had existed between the automobile industry and the oil industry. Who was going to pay for clearing the air? Until the Clean Air Act, the oil industry, being more sophisticated politically and having much more money, had basically succeeded in forcing the automobile companies and the consumers to pay the costs. Meanwhile, they have not done anything. Now that the playing field has been made more level, the costs are decreasing.

It is true that the cable industry was a big political supporter of President Bush. This fact was not lost on the Democrats, who sought to re-regulate, so the issue is related to the political process. Consequently, the networks were among those who were happiest at President Bush's defeat. I'm being a little provocative in making this point, but the cable bill and its veto were not irrelevant to President Bush. It goes right to the heart of the political process.

QUESTION: What was the role of Barbara Bush as first lady in the Bush administration, and how much influence did she have on the President and his decisions? Also, I have always been intrigued by why President Bush continued to keep John Sununu as his first chief of staff as long as he did only to chose a second chief of staff who turned out to be rather incompetent. Did these decisions contribute in any way to the demise of his presidency?

MR. GRAY: With regard to Mrs. Bush, she is remarkable. She is terrific as both a speaker and a mother. She is a remarkably civil person who helped set the tone for what I would like to think was a very civil, ethical, clean presidency. On matters of specific issues, she didn't have much to say and didn't want to say much, except in the field of education and on literacy, which was her pet charity. She was influential in elevating the issue of education. She was very supportive of me when I got into the brutal business on the Civil Rights Act. She understood that it was a slant on education, and I will forever be grateful for her support.

As for Sununu, his big mistake—which I believe was not a mistake, but a good thing—was his unwillingness to play the press

game the way it should be played. My father told the story of when
Jim Reston, then a correspondent for the Washington bureau of the
New York Times, took him to lunch while my father was undersecretary of the Army in 1949. Reston said, "You will be one of the
great stars of our generation—that's clear. For my part, I will be the
chronicler, the newspaper record, and we will make the history
books. We will write history for our generation and our children's
generation. I will make your place in history, and I will demand
only a few things in return—a little leaked document here, and
another there." To this proposed deal my father said, "I wasn't
brought up that way." His punishment was that he was never
mentioned in the *New York Times* for the next 30 years.

My father also refused to cooperate with Joseph Alsop and
consequently incurred Alsop's enmity—an enmity that lasted
throughout Joe Alsop's career. I once asked my father why Joe
Alsop was always mad at him, and he replied that it was because he
would not leak information to Alsop.

Sununu also refused to play that game, and the press will
punish anyone for that resolution. As a result, Sununu lost part of
his support base. He also did some stupid things with regard to his
travel. I begged him once to take the train to Philadelphia for some
event. I had determined that it would take less time to take the
train than fly there in a G-3, taking into account such time-
consuming elements as rush hour traffic. He wouldn't do it. The
next thing I knew he was off to a stamp auction in a limousine, and
that was it. His base of support was fragile; the press had many
ways to get at him, and that was his undoing.

NARRATOR: What about his successor?

MR. GRAY: There are some details with which I am not prepared
to go public yet. Samuel Skinner was decent. One of the problems
was that he took the job on a condition that was untenable—that the
campaign would be run exclusively outside of the building. That
model had been last followed when Ford lost and was not followed
when Nixon or Reagan won reelection. You can't let the campaign
go outside of the White House; thus, when James Baker came in
and took over, he brought it all back into the White House. It was
too late, I suppose, but that was the problem that made Skinner

look inept. He was being charged with or given accountability or responsibility for things totally beyond his control.

One reason that Bush lost and people didn't look good in the campaign is that we didn't have Lee Atwater. Had he survived, the outcome might have been different. Without him, the campaign people were without a leader. We just hadn't filled the vacuum. Skinner may have been able to help, but he was not allowed to do so. According to the arrangement, he would not have anything to say about politics.

QUESTION: Is it appropriate for the president's counsel to handle personal business for the president?

MR. GRAY: I think it is not appropriate. Personal business should be handled by a private lawyer, and the White House should be kept informed. For example, I could not be excluded from matters that involved the President. I was always consulted or informed on various issues. At the same time, I never had the ultimate decision-making authority with regard to personal matters.

QUESTION: The war on drugs and his education policy were two big items early in President Bush's administration. He addressed it in his State of the Union Address and the Governor's Conference on Education. Both items, however, seemed to lose their direction toward the end of the administration. Do you think the White House and the president were directed differently toward the end of his administration, and if so, why do you think that might have happened?

MR. GRAY: I don't think President Bush's interest in addressing the problem of drugs ever wavered. He had an articulate drug czar in the beginning—William Bennett, who later left; he is a hard act to follow. With Bennett's departure, it might have looked as if Bush were downgrading the war on drugs. It is almost inevitable that it would appear that way because no one is as good on the issues of education and drugs as Bill Bennett. I don't think the President ever wavered on the issue, even in terms of his appointees on the education side of it. Lamar Alexander was a very good secretary of education. He did a good job, and I think President Bush made some important headway on the education front.

Nine out of every ten dollars of public money spent on education is spent at the state level, not the federal level. The federal government can't really do much to force people to act differently. It is a bully pulpit more than a budgetary or regulatory matter. The President, with the help of Mrs. Bush's efforts at improving literacy, set the stage for the revolution now occurring at the state level of education. School choice initiatives are making headway everywhere. They are not supported by the Democrats because the Teachers Union, the most powerful education union and one of the most powerful building blocks of the Democratic party, is opposed to them. As a result, President Clinton, who is also very interested in education, is boxed with his own party on that issue. Nevertheless, enormous strides are being taken to clean up the educational system.

If I had more time, I would explain the relation of civil rights to education. President Bush both highlighted and addressed this relationship, although again, the press is so complicated that his message never got through in the press.

It might surprise you to know that until a couple of years ago, an employer could not use a diploma, let alone a transcript, to make hiring decisions. I'm not talking about universities that probably could not imagine admitting students without looking at transcripts. Employers were not permitted to rely on transcripts or diplomas. The only institution in America exempt from this ban was the military, which happily went along requiring diplomas as a condition of enlistment. About 99 percent of all of its enlistees are high school graduates.

President Bush eliminated that ban so that businesses now can ask for evidence of educational achievement and ability, thereby encouraging the schools to produce 75 percent of what the customers want; that is, employers will take 75 percent of the high school graduates who don't go on to college. I think President Bush made extraordinary strides in this area.

QUESTION: As White House counsel, were you ever called upon by President Bush to advise him on issues with regard to Iran-contra or Colonel North? Also, were you consulted in President Bush's appointment of Clarence Thomas to the Supreme Court, given all of the fire power brought to bear against that nomination?

MR. GRAY: I would like to use this opportunity to say something about Oliver North and his campaign for the Republican nomination for senator. I will do anything I can, even bribe you, but you have got to vote for Jim Miller. He is a fantastic guy and is as much of a Reaganite as Oliver North could ever pretend to be. In fact, Miller actually knew President Reagan and went to meetings with him. All of the meetings that North claimed to have attended is a fabrication. I can't say enough in support of Jim Miller. He deserves to be Virginia's Republican nominee; moreover, he could beat Chuck Robb. North doesn't have a prayer of beating Robb.

To return to your question, we were not prepared for the ruckus in response to Iran-contra. The investigation, led by independent counsel Lawrence Walsh, is a book or two books in itself. It was an extraordinary set of events and took seven years of my life to work on it.

A couple of points need to be made about Iran-contra that have gotten lost in the shuffle. Forget the fact that anyone was convicted for any wrongdoing prior to the investigation. You are supposed to lie to Congress afterwards. Not only was no one ever convicted of any wrongdoing, no one was ever even charged with doing anything wrong. Does everyone understand this point? North, Poindexter, Reagan, and Weinberger were never accused of doing anything wrong. There was no violation of law in selling arms to Iran.

There is some question about whether Congress was properly notified about the sales, an export control act, whether the Israelis had an end-user certificate, and so forth. President Reagan didn't violate anything except for his own policy of not dealing with terrorists, from which he can exempt himself.

As an end result, did we incite a new wave of terrorism with these arms sales? No, we did not. Instead, we opened a channel to the monarchs who are now in control, and relations are much better as a result.

On the contra side, we have peace, democracy, and free markets now in Nicaragua. We kicked the commies out! What is wrong with that? Did the Dole amendments really prohibit military aid to the contras? Not really. In fact, Congress really did not want to prohibit aid. They tried to have it both ways. Congress actually passed a secret law, unavailable to anyone without a security clearance, and thus the press could never write about it. They wanted to be able to say if we happened to lose the war that we had supported the contras. I get so angry about it because it was a shell game.

Consider humanitarian aid to the contras, for example. Isn't humanitarian aid to a guerilla force an oxymoron? Money is fungible. If they get boots, they can spend their hard-earned dollars on bullets. Congress was never trying to shut the contras down; they were pouring money into that area. Moreover, Congressman Edward Boland knew this. At one point on the House floor, he said that the total amount of money that Congress approved for humanitarian aid, the money that private citizens are sending there, and the money the Sultan of Brunei and the Saudis were contributing was more than what we had voted for in explicit aid. Congress knew the situation. Members made numerous visits there. We once compared the number of congressional people to the number of White House people—that is, political appointees, not military arms services people—who went to Nicaragua during the so-called Boland ban. Some 85 members of Congress made that trip, compared to only about 30 political appointees who went there during this critical period. For them to say they didn't know what was transpiring is ridiculous. Everyone knew.

In short, no law was ever violated, though people probably were not completely candid with Congress after the fact. I'm not sure that is a heinous crime. They were not candid with us. Why should we be candid with them? That is just the war between the branches, and it ought not be criminalized the way it was.

As for the Clarence Thomas nomination, that is another matter entirely. We were not prepared, but President Bush knew it would be difficult. When we went to Kennebunkport, the one thing Bush asked Thomas was, "Are you ready? Do you think you can handle the press?" Thomas replied, "Yes, I'm ready." Still, none of us had any idea it would come to the conclusion it did. My own view is that this incident was a replay of the Marcus Garvey affair in the 1920s. Marcus Garvey actually was a Jamaican, not an American. A spellbinding speaker and a great leader, he was an incredible threat to the NAACP-type approach toward dealing with race in America, which was why the NAACP had to frame him. They got him convicted and kicked out of the country. The jurors later said that he had been framed and was innocent. Any black historian will say that in terms of influence in American black history, Garvey ranks among the top five with Martin Luther King and Booker T. Washington. Nevertheless, he was framed, and everyone understood it to be so after the fact. I think they were doing the same thing to Clarence Thomas. He represented a streak of independence, self-help, and an "I want to do this on my own-I'm not going to claim group victimization"-type of mentality. This threat to the existing civil rights leadership was real, so they tried to frame him—only this time, they lost.

One thing I would encourage people to do is watch the black sitcom being produced by Norman Lear that is modeled after Clarence Thomas's EEOC (Equal Employment Opportunity Commission) public affairs director, a man named Armstrong Williams, who has a very popular black talk show in Washington. This man is an extraordinary fellow and is the model and consultant for the sitcom, which is about a conservative black young man who fights his liberal parents. This show could have a major impact on the culture regarding how these issues are addressed.

Armstrong Williams told me that one of the first intellectual battles he had with Hollywood was over Clarence Thomas and whether the protagonist, the hero in the story, would be seen as supporting Clarence Thomas. The Hollywood scriptwriters naturally wrote down that he was going to be opposed. How could one possibly be in favor of Clarence Thomas? Quite a battle ensued, and Armstrong Williams took it all the way to Norman Lear, who then checked it out and reluctantly decided that the protagonist had to support Clarence Thomas. This instance will be the first time Hollywood has come out in favor of Clarence Thomas.

Thomas has recently again been misinterpreted. In an article in the *New Yorker*, the press now writes about how Thomas is moping around, depressed, and won't talk to anyone. It is total hogwash! He is having a great time. I saw him at a wedding of one of my former assistants, and he was in great form. This story about how he is totally cut off from the world is total hogwash. A fault line exists in America about how blacks are viewed. In my opinion, the principal reason Thomas was so strongly opposed and why they framed him in this way was because he was so intellectually and strongly committed against quotas and rights based on groups rather than individuals.

One interesting thing is that at his confirmation, Congress didn't ask him more than one or two questions about quotas because the Democrats didn't want to have a black man opposing quotas on national television. As a result, they let him pass on that issue, although that is the reason they went after him. My own view is that Thomas is going to make a great Supreme Court justice. Moreover, he is breaking the color barrier in much the same way that Jackie Robinson did in baseball and is making it much easier for the Colin Powells and others to succeed.

I have a story to tell that may seem unrelated, but it is a true story. It is thirdhand to me and thus will be fourthhand to you. Colin Powell, who is also Jamaican, was the commencement speaker at Harvard last year. I was told that after Powell was selected, there was rearguard action to derail him and have Al Gore substituted in his place because it was thought that Powell would irritate the sensibilities of the gay community at Harvard. I don't think that was the real reason. I think the liberal part of this movement didn't want to celebrate a black who is, at best, moderate. On the bottom of every letter Powell sends to a kid who asks him what his prescription for success is, he writes in his own handwriting, "Stay in school." That, however, is not the advice that many in leadership give. To them, Colin Powell is politically incorrect. They tried to derail him, and it backfired. In the end, he remained the commencement speaker and got standing ovations every five seconds. The gays showed protest by standing with their backs to him, but there was no scene. It was an incredible success. This story reflects the difficulty prominent blacks have to face in our culture to really have success. It is hard to describe and articulate, but a parallel exists between the effort to try to derail Powell's speakership and the effort to derail Clarence Thomas.

NARRATOR: We think you very much for a spirited and candid discussion and look forward to your next visit.

CHAPTER 2

ORGANIZING FOR POLICY-MAKING*

EDWARD J. DERWINSKI

NARRATOR: Edward J. Derwinski has had a long and distinguished career in public service, both in the executive and the legislative branches. He began his political career as a member of the Illinois state legislature. He was later elected to 12 terms as congressman from the Fourth District in Illinois and served on a number of congressional committees. He was ranking member of the Foreign Affairs Committee in three Congresses and from 1974–83 was ranking member of the Post Office and Civil Service Committee. Mr. Derwinski was executive committee member and then chairman of the U.S. congressional delegation to the International Parliamentarian Union. He holds a bachelor of science degree from Loyola University in Chicago and he served in the U.S. Army in World War II.

Mr. Derwinski was administrator of the Veterans Administration (VA) and then, at Cabinet rank, secretary of veterans affairs. Before that, he had served as counselor to the Department of State and then undersecretary for Security Assistance, Science and Technology.

He has unique insights into both the Reagan and Bush administrations. As you may know, he was one of two people who left the Bush administration at the request of the President. The leadership of the Veterans of Foreign Wars (VFW) warned that

Presented in a Forum at the Miller Center of Public Affairs on 9 February 1993.

they could not support the Bush presidential reelection campaign if Ed Derwinski remained VA administrator. Mr. Derwinski has made it clear that it was only the VFW leadership that raised this issue and not the general membership as such.

The statement I found most revealing about Mr. Derwinski was made by Senator Alan Simpson while this controversy was occurring. As Senator Simpson put it, Derwinski was not a high visibility member of the Bush Cabinet, but he was a good soldier, the ultimate team player. Apparently, all through this controversy Mr. Derwinski stayed in close contact with Senator Simpson, who is a pretty good man to have on your side. We welcome Mr. Derwinski's comments on the Bush presidency.

MR. DERWINSKI: At the risk of a slight exaggeration, my association with George Bush began in January 1967. He was a freshman congressman and I was then coming into my fifth term. In those days seniority was respected. Mr. Bush came from Texas, and it was a rarity in those days to have a Republican from Texas. The first day George came into what we call the "cloak room," which is the area behind the House chamber, and asked me for directions to the men's room. I told him it was the second door on the left. He found it and has been grateful to me ever since.

I can tell you an interesting story that also shows the trend of politics. I first came to Congress in January 1959. At that time, there wasn't a single Republican U.S. senator from the Old South, and there were only about eight Republican congressmen from the 11 historically Confederate states, two of whom were from Virginia—Joel Broyhill, who represented Arlington, Alexandria, and the suburbs of Washington, and Dick Poff, who I think represented a district from Richmond. There was one Republican from the hills of western North Carolina and two from districts in East Tennessee adjacent to North Carolina. My recollection of Civil War history is that people in those hill areas were Yankee sympathizers. For that reason, since the end of the Civil War, there have been Republican House members from those areas. We picked up one or two House seats in the South along the way, but in 1964 the Goldwater campaign was a disaster for the Republicans.

A breakthrough took place in 1964. New Republican congressmen were elected in South Carolina, Alabama, and Mississippi. In 1966 Mr. Bush was one of more than a dozen new Republican

House members who came out of the South. The Republican party made a special effort to accommodate what they saw as the wave of the future, granting legitimacy to the Republican party in the South. To consolidate this new power base, they decided that they needed to have a Texan on the Ways and Means Committee, so George Bush was chosen to serve. This combination of geography and power politics demonstrated to the Texas oil interests that Republicans were as good for them as Democrats. With a Texan Republican on the Ways and Means Committee the oil industry would not be beholden only to Texas Democrats.

It was done openly; politics were handled in a frank and practical manner in those days. The seniority system was still in place; so was the rule that a freshman was to be seen and not heard. If you were reelected and came back as a second-termer, you became an accepted force. Bush followed that procedure and was beginning to work his way up. In 1970, however, he ran for the Senate and lost to Lloyd Bentsen. As a reward for his heroic effort against Bentsen, Bush was given the position of ambassador to the United Nations, where he served for two years.

George Bush did an effective job at the United Nations. He brought a congressional and a natural American style to representing the United States at the United Nations. By that I mean he wasn't a diplomat and therefore didn't conduct himself like the classical, professional diplomat. The 101 course for American career diplomats is to study how British diplomats behave and act accordingly. George Bush came in with an acquired Texas style, however. He didn't act like a Connecticut socialite; he acted like a breezy Texan. In his speeches to committees and to the General Assembly at the United Nations he used an eloquent, oratorical style, even though U.N. speeches almost never change votes. For the most part, delegates at the United Nations have been instructed by their home foreign ministry on how they should vote on a certain issue. Nevertheless, Bush became known for his eloquent style of oratory. In this way, he energized and inspired the normally staid U.S. mission to become much more active.

In those days the ambassador to the United Nations had Cabinet status. Theoretically, the ambassador to the United Nations should take his or her orders from the secretary of state just as any other ambassador in the direct chain of command would.

In 1960, the Democrats had a bitter convention in which Kennedy received the nomination, although Adlai Stevenson had hoped to be the candidate again. There was a solid group of Stevenson loyalists in the Democratic party, so as a gesture of goodwill, after Kennedy was elected, he appointed Adlai Stevenson as ambassador to the United Nations. In a move of great internal diplomacy, he also announced that because Mr. Stevenson was a man of such great stature, he would be afforded Cabinet status. This wonderful gesture of putting Mr. Stevenson in New York, where he couldn't do any damage to the Kennedy administration, was simply practical politics. At the same time, the U.N. ambassador would come down whenever possible to attend Cabinet meetings, even though his own boss, the secretary of state, would be there too.

As a result, all subsequent U.S. ambassadors to the United Nations inherited Cabinet status, including George Bush. Interestingly, one of the first things he did in his presidency was to gracefully drop the U.N. ambassador from Cabinet status. Having seen it from an inside vantage point, George Bush realized that such a status wasn't necessary. Meanwhile, I came in as secretary of veterans affairs, formerly the Veterans Administration, which had just been elevated from an agency to a Cabinet department, so they had a seat for me at the Cabinet table as well.

How did President Bush organize the White House? He didn't; the White House was organized by John Sununu. Governor Sununu was a strong administrator and an excellent chief of staff until he ran afoul of the media and stumbled as the result of a number of personal and semiofficial behavior patterns. He did have the President's confidence, however. Unlike President Carter, who organized and ran his own White House in a meticulous way—there were stories that Mr. Carter used to approve the list of people who could use the White House tennis courts—Bush didn't bother with those kinds of details. He immediately gravitated to foreign policy.

My relations within the administration were good. I am watching the Clinton administration carefully to see if the pattern we established will remain. For the first couple of weeks, we met at 10:00 a.m. every Tuesday and Thursday. Then we began meeting only once a week for about three months, and after that every other week. The longer the administration continued, the more time there was between Cabinet meetings.

The reasons for this were twofold. First, the Cabinet doesn't act like a board of directors; the Cabinet makes no decisions at all. I can't recall in the four years of the Bush presidency that Bush ever said, "Raise your hands and let's vote on the subject."   Basically, the Cabinet was a sounding board. We were given a briefing on any immediate crisis on the domestic or international front, but we were not a decision-making body as such. Second, the tendency was that once every Cabinet secretary began to gain control of his or her department, they went directly to the President, through Mr. Sununu, if they had a problem. The only time the President intervened was when there was a dispute between two departments and he was called upon to be a referee.

At the VA, for example, we had a natural overlap in health issues with Health and Human Services (HHS). We also had a natural overlap with the Department of Defense. Early in the administration I sat down with Mr. Cheney and Dr. Sullivan on separate occasions to review what we had inherited. Only minor structural changes were required, and we were able to proceed in a normal manner. There were no situations in which Mr. Bush had to referee. We also had some contacts with the Department of Education, since the VA administered the G.I. Bill. We also worked with Housing and Urban Development (HUD) in trying to initiate a special housing program for homeless veterans. These cooperative efforts were very successful.

The only battles with other departments of government were fought indirectly, and they involved the budget. If you wanted to squeeze a billion dollars from the budget, someone else had to relinquish that amount. Those debates were intense, but they took place behind the scenes at the Office of Management and Budget.

The White House staff—whatever the ideology of the administration—is much larger than it appears on paper, in terms of actual working people. Every department and agency is required to provide staff support for the White House. Agency heads either send a couple of people to work in the Old Executive Office Building who remain on the agency's payroll, or, as in most cases, one or two people would work for the White House but remain housed in the various departments of government.

Part of the reason for this is that occasionally the White House has to fend off an irate congressman who is trying to cut the White House budget for political reasons. By spreading the personnel around the government, the White House receives the support it needs without having to go through an annual battle with Congress over the precise number of the political staff.

Everyone in the White House is pretty much free to bestow a title on himself or herself, and Clinton's new administration is no different. There seem to be hundreds of people with the title of "special assistant to the president," even though they might work there for four years and never meet the president. This glorified and egocentric collection of minor functionaries resembles the classical courts of old Europe. The problem of getting to see the president is no different than it must have been 500 years ago in England when you had to pierce the army of people surrounding the monarch.

One of the problems I encountered was gaining access to the President. I didn't mind Mr. Sununu calling me and asking for the reason for my requested visit so that the President could be briefed and an appointment time could be scheduled. But when some 15th junior "special assistant" to the President called, I would draw the line. As a Cabinet officer, I had to cut through that maze, which I usually did by going directly to Mr. Sununu.

Did the President take command of the bureaucracy? The answer is yes and no. Mr. Sununu ran the President's own bureaucracy, and I assume the President was pleased with that arrangement. But I'll tell you frankly that when Mr. Sununu left and Mr. Skinner came in, the White House bureaucracy collapsed. For the last year, the White House was often malfunctioning because unlike the completely self-confident and decisive Mr. Sununu, Mr. Skinner agonized 24 hours a day over decisions. As a result, the White House suffered a slow paralysis from the moment Sununu left and Skinner came in. When Baker took over at the end of August, it was too late to stop the White House's internal collapse.

As far as getting control of the government bureaucracy, Mr. Bush did a good job, as one would expect, given his experience. He had served for two terms in the House, two years as U.S. ambassador to the United Nations, a year-and-a-half as ambassador to the People's Republic of China, and two years as chairman of the Republican National Committee. Thus, he knew the government from several different angles and was able to closely observe the Reagan administration as vice president for eight years. Whenever we appealed to President Bush for a decision, he was on top of the subject and on top of the issues. To that extent, I would say that he *did* take charge of the bureaucracy.

One of the great frustrations of the presidency is not being able to use personnel wisely. The federal civil service structure is so protective that no president or administration is ever comfortable with trying to manage the bureaucracy. A curse of bureaucracy is the built-in ability to consistently procrastinate. My one rule as secretary of veterans affairs was that at the end of a meeting, a decision had to be made. After ensuring that all people involved had been heard, I would make a decision. I found that this was one way to handle the bureaucracy.

It is much tougher for the president, however, because he is not aware of the constant battles within departments, especially if there is a secretary in a department who isn't making decisions. Decision making is extremely difficult in the federal government because the structure is top-heavy, and there is a natural resistance of the careerist to decisions made by the political appointees. In turn, political appointees take a dubious view of the careerist, which is understandable. A careerist is more cooperative if you keep him or her informed, and they will do what you ask of them. In too many departments the cleavage between the careerist and the political appointee is endless. It is already showing up in the early months of the new administration.

Under President Bush, relations between the White House and Cabinet-level departments were very good. We were told to deal with an officer called the Cabinet secretary, who was responsible for setting the agenda for Cabinet meetings as well as for dealing with any other requests we made, such as the occasional perks. These included the occasional use of the president's box at the Kennedy Center and visits to Camp David to work and socialize with fellow Cabinet officers. These visits worked very well in keeping everyone in touch with each other.

Mr. Sununu, who had developed a reputation as something of a monster, was in fact an amazingly pleasant gentleman. He is a certified genius with a very high IQ, however, and geniuses are difficult people. He instinctively makes decisions quickly, and once he made a decision it was difficult to sway him. When I went to see him with a proposal and he made an immediate decision, I would say, "Wait a minute; I've only given you one side. Give me two or three more minutes and I will give you the other side." I would never let him make an immediate decision but would always give him the pros and cons in an attempt to slow down his decision-making process so I would have some maneuvering room at the end. This worked out fairly well.

Because we had surprisingly few turf fights, relations at the Cabinet level were most agreeable. I will explain one exception, however, because it has a human nature side to it. One of the biggest headaches I inherited was the issue of veterans' exposure to Agent Orange, which was used as a defoliant in Vietnam. There was a great debate that still continues in the scientific community as to how significant that exposure may have been to the health of the servicemen. When I left Congress six years earlier, the issue was already boiling. During my six years at the State Department I was rather isolated from mundane problems in Washington because I was moving in the exalted areas of foreign policy.

When I moved to the Veterans Administration, I found that the Agent Orange issue was as troublesome as ever, so I innocently decided to resolve it. After reviewing cases where the medical records seemed to show a pattern of ailments connected with service in Southeast Asia, I decided to give all of these veterans a service-connected disability. By coincidence, a group of veterans had a case pending at that point in a U.S. court in San Francisco. The court reached a similar decision that where there was a pattern of physical ailments on record, the VA should acknowledge that they were related to service in Vietnam.

I held a press conference and announced that we were accepting the court's decision and that we were not going to appeal it. I was not aware that it wasn't my announcement or decision to make, and for some reason my counsel general didn't tell me otherwise. Not being a lawyer, I was only vaguely aware of an official called the solicitor general, who is the government's legal representative in cases in the federal court system.

The next thing I knew, I received a frantic call from the deputy attorney general saying that I had to rescind my decision. By this time 48 hours had passed, and every major newspaper in the country was editorializing on the wonderful Bush administration and its "points of light," one of which was finally doing the right thing for Vietnam veterans. I told the deputy attorney general, "Fine with me. You make the announcement; you be the S.O.B! I have made my decision. You go ahead and announce that you are going to appeal because the solicitor general prefers to appeal every decision."

Obviously, this became a crisis. Mr. Thornburg was then attorney general, and he wasn't aware of the issue until someone handed him a newspaper. He called me to ask that I step back. I said, "No, Dick, *you* do it. I'm the good guy. If you want to be the bad guy, you make an announcement that as attorney general, you are overriding the secretary of veteran affairs and that you are not going to be magnanimous to these veterans."

The next day we went to see John Sununu. In his wisdom, he looked the situation over, smiled, and said to me, "You shouldn't have done that. You are absolutely wrong. The solicitor general is correct; the attorney general is correct. But everyone likes your decision, so we won't change it. The next time, ask the attorney general before you do anything." That is how easily the situation was resolved.

Regarding President Bush's relations with Congress, I would say they were good on the surface but horrible beneath the surface. All former members have a fraternal relationship with Congress, but since the Congress was controlled by the Democrats, they never really gave President Bush as much cooperation as he deserved. This is the way the American political system works. President Bush spent four frustrating years trying to work with the Democratic-controlled Congress, while on the surface there was always a wonderful camaraderie.

As an old congressman, I had the same experience. When I went before committees for a hearing, I would first receive extravagant eulogies, then I would suddenly get a stilleto in my back on some budget item. Congressmen would shake your hand and slap you on the back, but you had to do battle with them during hearings. Thus, our relations with Congress were good as a whole, but working relations deteriorated over the four years.

Mr. Clinton will face the same problem—only it will be a little more difficult. The Democrats in Congress will have to find parochial, regional, or other reasons to differ with the administration. For example, don't cut the defense budget if it means 5,000 General Dynamics workers in Dallas will be laid off. As a former congressman and as vice president, Mr. Bush had a good feel for legislative affairs. This issue was natural and instinctive for him, so he paid close attention to it and kept up to date in that respect.

I can only give you a few instances of how and why the President made his choices of Cabinet members. It is obvious that he had an early understanding whereby Mr. Baker could take whatever Cabinet position he wanted. Having already been secretary of the treasury, Mr. Baker was probably interested in becoming either attorney general or secretary of state. I'm sure the process of choosing Mr. Baker as secretary of state was directed by Baker himself.

Secretary Brady was a Yale or prep-school classmate and trusted confidante of Mr. Bush, as far as I know. Brady had an excellent background on Wall Street, so he was a logical choice for secretary of the treasury. Mr. Thornburg had been in the Cabinet under President Reagan, and he was retained. The secretary of education had just been appointed 18 months before, and he was also retained. Everyone else was new. There were other logical appointments. For instance, Clayton Yeutter was by background a farm economist, so he became secretary of agriculture. Mr. Lujan was from New Mexico and served on the House Interior Committee in his 20 years in Congress, so he was a logical choice for interior secretary.

Then there was the problem of Senator John Tower's nomination to be secretary of defense, which ran into a buzz saw largely of his own making. Mr. Cheney then came in, which turned out to be a fortunate move. Cheney did a great job. Mr. Skinner came in as transportation secretary. He had the background expertise of having run the Metropolitan Transit District in Chicago.

I was probably the exception to the rule. All of my experience with the VA was as a congressman, handling complaints and casework from veterans. After my six years at the State Department, there were moments when I allowed my ego to run away with me, and I decided that I would be the logical choice for secretary of state. Mr. Baker had the pole position, however.

I received a call from President Bush asking me if I would be the VA secretary. He said that this would be a tough job. Since you don't refuse a president when he asks you to serve in his Cabinet, I gladly said yes. The job was indeed difficult, as the President stated, because some constituencies—such as farmers and veterans—are never satisfied.

Brent Scowcroft, who directed the National Security Council, was an unusually fascinating gentleman. He is a *bona fide* general and West Point alumnus, but clearly a back-room strategist. He was perfect for the NSC because he is thoughtful, thorough, pragmatic, and intensely loyal. He was perfect in both personality and background for this key position. Presidents need someone who is extremely objective and understands that he is there to serve the president and give him the best information he can.

The man who will be remembered in political history as one of the most controversial Bush appointees is Mr. Richard Darman at the Office of Management and Budget. He is generally blamed by Republicans for the demise of the Bush administration because of the 1990 tax deal, which undermined the President's pledge of "Read my lips: no new taxes." It turned out that there *were* new taxes. Mr. Darman also kept telling the President that prosperity was just around the corner and the next quarter's economic statistics would be much better. When they finally did improve, they were six months too late, and Mr. Bush floundered in large measure because of the public perception of the administration's lack of attention to the economy.

At every Cabinet meeting for four years, Mr. Darman said without fail, "Next month's reports are going to be better"; or "Next quarter's statistics are going to be better." In some Republican circles in Washington Mr. Darman is considered the evil monster of the Bush team.

The President also had an economic adviser, Dr. Mike Boskin, who was a UCLA professor, a classical, ivory-tower economist. Unfortunately, he gave the President the same type of advice that Darman did. According to the charts, we were doing two-tenths of 1 percent better than Carter did in the same month in his presidency, and next month we were going to do one-tenth of one percent better.

Let me digress a moment to say that, of necessity, there are times in the Washington political process when little games are played, especially in dealing with Congress. I can give you an innocent example from my tenure at the State Department. We were always a little tight budgetwise, especially in foreign aid. We would always come up with recommendations in the area of foreign aid, aimed at pleasing the State Department constituency, which were the different nations around the world.

Congress had a list of countries it wished to serve. For example, no matter what we at the State Department offered as the aid package for Israel, Congress would always add to it. For domestic political purposes, certain congressmen had to do something special for Israel. Thus, the State Department always quoted a lower figure for Israel than they needed or wanted, knowing that Congress would raise it. Likewise, the State Department would always request a much higher figure for Pakistan than we knew would survive Congress because of the human rights problems that have existed there for years. In the end, when Congress made its cut, we pretty much got what we needed.

With that little waltz in mind, I looked at the history of VA funding. I found that during the Reagan years, the administration's budget directors would always propose low figures for the Veterans Administration, knowing that Congress would raise them. I decided that was poor politics because it gave Congress the credit in the eyes of the veterans. I told Darman up front that I wanted an increase of $1.25 billion. He said they could only give us $400 million and Congress could give us the balance. I said, "No, I want it the other way. I want the President to give us so much money that Congress won't be able to afford to give more and then *we* will be the heroes." This is just practical politics.

When the figures came back from OMB, there was Mr. Darman's $400 million increase instead of the $1.25 billion I had asked for. I asked to see the President, which displeased Mr. Darman. As I was on my way to see the President, Mr. Darman grabbed me and said, "I'll give you more money; don't make an issue of it." Well, I had been around long enough to have experience in such matters, so I explained to the President in very practical terms why we had to provide the money up front.

The President understood the situation and said that was the way it would be. For the next three years, I had no battles with Mr. Darman. We would estimate the maximum that Congress would appropriate and then use that as our figure. Last year we proposed a budget increase of $1.3 billion; Congress added a mere $18 million.

President Bush's main strength was that he was an amazingly fine, decent, and wonderful human being with an exceptionally charming first lady. Barbara Bush was probably the most popular first lady since Mamie Eisenhower. He did have weaknesses, however.

One weakness was natural and has been perennial throughout history; presidents, kings, and prime ministers all fall in love with foreign policy, which is where the glamour, excitement, and romance are. It is much more interesting wandering around the world, visiting foreign heads of states or receiving heads of states at the White House and discussing issues of the world than it is to attempt to solve sticky domestic issues.

This is not only true of U.S. presidents, but of foreign leaders such as Mr. Yeltsin in Russia. Here is a country whose internal transportation system is so decrepit that half the crops they produce rot in the fields, and he spends much of his time traveling around the world discussing foreign-policy problems. It is his way of escaping the awesome headaches of unsolvable domestic problems. Likewise, even though Prime Minister Mulroney of Canada currently "enjoys" a mere 20 percent approval rating, he was the last man to see Bush before he left office, and he was the first head of state to visit Clinton. It's much easier to be in Washington talking about world affairs than in Ottawa trying to solve a budget deficit.

Of course, the President's strength clearly was foreign policy. With his expertise and background at the State Department and as vice president, he had a feel for it and did a great job. He was the acknowledged world leader. His weakness was the perception that he didn't address domestic issues.

I can't speak for how Mr. Bush will be judged in the future by historians, but contemporary journalists have already made a judgment. In foreign policy they gave him an A+, ranking him along with FDR and Eisenhower; in domestic policy, however, they gave him a C-. History will probably treat him in this way. He performed exceptionally well as the world leader, but unfortunately the *perception*—as opposed to actual accomplishments—on the domestic front was much poorer, and that was a factor in the recent campaign.

In evaluating the contribution of the President's associates, I would agree with most of the analyses in saying that everyone—aside from Mr. Darman—performed in the good-to-outstanding range.

There were some appointees who had impossible assignments. Carla Hills was our special trade representative. She is absolutely brilliant, but she faced an impossible task. There is no immediate solution to the complications of protectionism around the world. There were other "mission impossibles." How can the secretary of agriculture fix a system in which some farmers are paid to grow crops and others are paid not to grow them?

How does the secretary of the interior respond to a terrible split between farmers out west, who want more dams to irrigate more land and produce more fruits and vegetables for society, versus environmentalists who want all of the rivers of the country running as clean and pure as they did 500 years ago? There are certain no-win situations. Cabinet officers are judged by the end results of their efforts, but because they inherit structural problems that can't be solved in three or four years, their results often reflect expedient compromises.

One example I can give of a no-win situation happened to me personally. I was asked to leave the Cabinet just before the 1992 election because the organized veterans were unhappy with me and threatened to vote against Mr. Bush. I therefore left the Cabinet to placate them. The issue that provoked this situation involved use of the 173 veterans' hospitals, which operate at about 60 percent of capacity, since most veterans nowadays are treated on an outpatient basis. Due to declining use, these hospitals are now underutilized.

Dr. Louis Sullivan and I decided to conduct a test whereby the Department of Health and Human Services (HHS) would refer patients from public health clinics to three VA hospitals. HHS would pay for their hospital costs. The veterans would continue to receive priority, but we would use available space for under-privileged nonveterans. The three areas where hospitals were chosen for this test were in Salem, Virginia, for the underprivileged in the Appalachia region; Tuskegee, Alabama, a 100 percent black community in which a private hospital was closed approximately six years ago; and either South Dakota or Wyoming, where a VA hospital adjacent to an Indian reservation would be used for Indians in need of medical care. Payment would be made by HHS for any extra staff needed to serve the new workload. We planned to test this idea for three years.

The veterans groups became very upset. They felt it was a sacrilege to allow nonveterans into a veterans' hospital. Before long I was being hung in effigy in every VFW clubhouse in the country. Yet everyone to whom I explained this situation would say it was a good idea and every editorial we had was supportive. Even the *Washington Post*, which isn't normally supportive of Republican administrations, ran a lead editorial saying it was a wonderful idea.

We would have served a great humanitarian need and also protected the VA hospitals from the scrutiny of some health reformer who would point out that since they were operating under practical capacity, we should close some of them.

This controversy arose at about the time the campaign was starting, and soon the campaign advisers panicked. The VFW leaders stated that if Bush were to get rid of Derwinski, they would endorse him. Therefore, I left. They double-crossed President Bush, however, and didn't endorse him.

My point is that this was a no-win situation. Ten or fifteen years from now we will have to initiate a program such as the one I proposed to justify keeping the VA hospitals open, or we will have to close those that are operating far below capacity. We were attempting to tell our veterans that the hospitals must be used more fully or else they would be lost. Politically, the situation occurred at the wrong time, when the administration was going downhill during an election year. This is a classic case of a good decision that was bad in terms of politics. It is also an example of a pressure group that shoots itself in the foot today and will suffer from it 15 years from now.

Australia has a system similar to the one I proposed. They also built a system of veterans' hospitals after World Wars I and II, and today 40 percent of their patients are veterans and 60 percent are from the rest of their society. As a result, their veterans hospitals are full and will stay open.

If the last election had been held two days after Desert Storm, President Bush would have won by acclamation. Likewise, if the campaign had happened this spring with all of the economic indicators going up, he probably would have been reelected. Problems of timing undermined what I believe was a good, solid, responsible administration.

QUESTION: The alleged Clinton passport scandal created an interesting bureaucratic problem. There were allegations that Bush appointees in the State Department were trying to disclose some damaging information from Governor Clinton's passport file. Clinton had been governor of Arkansas for a number of years, so he probably never had a security clearance. It seems to me that if one is running for president, this sort of information, if it exists, *should* be disclosed. Do you agree?

MR. DERWINSKI: As partisan as I am—instinctively combative in politics, having survived the Daley machine in Chicago in my early years—I thought that this was a non-issue from the start. First, it was 20-some years old. Second, the charge unfairly implied that Clinton's presence in Moscow during the Vietnam War could have somehow been subversive.

I don't agree with what Clinton did in regard to Vietnam. I think it is a shame that we have a draft dodger as President of the United States. Having made that statement, I see absolutely no reason why his trip to Moscow, which thousands of other Americans made in that period, should have had any bearing on the election. I was in Moscow in 1970 with a group of congressmen. The Soviets were good at attracting people to Moscow for tours lasting only a few days; they knew that if people stayed longer they would begin to see the social problems.

I thought the passport incident was a non-issue, and I thought it was clumsily handled by the State Department and the White House. By this time I had left the Veterans Administration and was working for the Bush campaign. They asked me to organize the ethnic groups I was working with to demand an investigation of Clinton's travels. I said no, and furthermore, if asked by the media, I would say it was a silly issue because thousands of other Americans traveled to Moscow in the same period.

I would like to make one other polite comment about politics. Notwithstanding the impact of television and the new style of campaigning with the use of negative advertisement, voters are pretty much predictable. They begin making up their minds about three weeks before an election, and as election day approaches, fewer people are undecided. Thus, by about the third week of October, the mind-set of the electorate was already in position. I felt that the issue wasn't one for which Mr. Clinton should have been criticized, and from a pragmatic standpoint, it didn't affect the election.

QUESTION: Weren't there rumors that Mr. Clinton renounced his American citizenship during the Vietnam War?

MR. DERWINSKI: There was never any proof of that. At Republican campaign headquarters, we were waiting for two things to appear—another mistress or a couple of illegitimate children in the hills of Arkansas. Then the issue about Clinton renouncing his citizenship came up. These are examples of the kind of silly, wild rumors that raise hopes in the excitement of a campaign. I remember in 1964, when I was a campaign manager for Barry Goldwater in Illinois, coming into headquarters about a week before the election and finding the staff jumping for joy, saying we were going to win the election because Billy Graham was going to endorse Goldwater. Billy Graham did not endorse Mr. Goldwater. We live through such rumors during every campaign.

NARRATOR: Would you say that the Bush campaign was poorly managed?

MR. DERWINSKI: That is an understatement. The two people who ran Bush's reelection campaign were not good politicians. One was a statistician and the other was an administrator, and neither one felt or understood the pulse of public opinion.

Another factor I discussed earlier was the White House staff and the people who work there. After Desert Storm, everyone in the White House was making plans to be working six more years. They also thought that they themselves had planned Desert Storm. There were many runaway egos. When the polls showed the President at 85 percent in public support, the complacency and smugness were shocking, and they never shook it off. They never understood that it was possible to be beaten.

I'm not a believer in negative campaigns, even though I come from Chicago where we play tough politics. I thought the Bush administration was good enough to have run a reelection campaign on everything that he had done right without having to spend 90 percent of its time bashing Clinton on the draft issue, which his Democrat opponents had done in the primary without hurting him politically. Who were we to think it was going to work in the fall campaign? They should have just sold George Bush and not spent all of our time bashing Bill Clinton. A change in tactics might have changed the psychology of the campaign.

QUESTION: You have observed this legislative and administrative process for a long time. How would you gauge some of the changes?

MR. DERWINSKI: In the old Congress there was obviously too much power vested in chairmen. The tendency to stifle debate also existed, and some of the votes weren't on the record. Those were weaknesses in the old process.

The new Congress as it is now constituted is unmanageable and ineffective for the simple reason that there is little party loyalty. Senators are seldom elected based on their party affiliation. The party line becomes a technical vehicle for election. They raise their own money, conduct their own campaigns, and are beholden only to their contributors—not to the party institutions.

The same thing is true in the House of Representatives. In some campaigns this year House members have spent $3-4 million getting elected. In the old days party loyalty and discipline were considered virtues, but it is difficult to impose those qualities on 535 self-proclaimed individual success stories in the House and Senate.

The role of seniority has ended for the most part. Seniority was not a particularly democratic procedure, but it had the advantage in that by the time you reached the top, you had enough experience to be fairly effective. If you were an ineffective individual, the system allowed for the number two or number three member to become the de facto leader. I discovered this practice early on in Congress with a couple of old chairmen who were there long beyond their effective years. But even in such cases, there was a degree of discipline and respect for that seniority. The understanding was that as freshmen, we were to be seen and not heard. The first thing you were told was not to bother making speeches— other members were not going to listen to you and your zeal to reform the world. If you were reelected and thus proved that you belonged in Congress, then the others would begin to listen to you.

When I first came to Congress 36 years ago, I asked some of the old-timers how to organize a legislative office. Without exception, the first thing they said was that I should get an efficient case worker to serve my constituents, because we are here to serve. Nowadays the first person a new congressman hires is a press aide. This difference reveals a great deal about the new mind-set.

QUESTION: Is there any hope for improving the quality of management in our bureaucratic system of government?

MR. DERWINSKI: The inefficiency of the federal structure is deplorable. Our government is too large, too cumbersome, and too rigid. I don't want to sound harsh, but the trouble with the federal government is that the typical federal worker is so well protected by civil service regulations that he or she doesn't have to do much more than go through the motions in their jobs. As a result, there is a sluggish, lethargic bureaucracy that is inherently wasteful.

The only way to cure this would be provocative. Layers of protection would have to be stripped away, which is dangerous because top-level judgment as to whether an individual should continue in service may not be fair and objective.

The typical federal employee joins the bureaucracy to have a safe career and then retire with a good pension. Certainly, there has to be some way to give them such protection and security. At the same time, however, the bureaucracy must be reminded that the customer is always right and that they are there to serve the American public.

I used to visit the VA hospitals unannounced. I would try to check into a hospital, for example, to observe how the admissions clerk would function. I found that among federal employees, there was a sense that the customer—the taxpayer—is less important than the bureaucrat's parochial interests. The bureaucracy must be streamlined and energized without turning it into a political spoils system. This remains an enormous challenge for government.

NARRATOR: Thank you, Mr. Derwinski, for your thought-provoking forum. We have been much enlightened during this session and appreciate your candid and forthright presentation.

II

GOVERNANCE AND THE
BUSH PRESIDENCY

CHAPTER 3

ACCOMPLISHMENTS AND SETBACKS*

CLAYTON YEUTTER

NARRATOR: We are honored to have Clayton Yeutter with us at the Miller Center today. Mr. Yeutter was born in Eustis, Nebraska. He attended the University of Nebraska where he earned his bachelor's degree, his law degree, and his doctoral degree in agricultural economics. He holds many honorary degrees, including degrees from the University of Nebraska, Georgetown, Maryland, and Clemson.

Mr. Yeutter has practiced law in Lincoln, Nebraska, and will soon be practicing in Washington. He has served on the boards of a number of companies, including Texas Instruments, Caterpillar, and Oppenheimer Funds, and has been president and chief executive officer of the Chicago Mercantile Exchange.

Clayton Yeutter is also a farmer and has managed the farming, ranching, and feeding operation on his farm in Nebraska. His early career included five years of service in the U.S. Air Force. He also taught at the University of Nebraska. Among his public services as an academician, he headed the University of Nebraska's mission to Colombia, where he led a technical assistance operation that was funded by various U.S. agencies.

His political and public service career began as chief of staff to the governor of Nebraska from 1966 to 1968. He joined the Department of Agriculture in 1970 when Clifford Hardin was

---

Presented in a Forum at the Miller Center of Public Affairs on 30 April 1993.

secretary of agriculture. Mr. Yeutter served in various capacities with the U.S. Department of Agriculture as administrator of the Consumer and Marketing Services, as assistant secretary in the same area, and also as assistant secretary (now undersecretary) for International Affairs and Commodity Programs.

From 1975 to 1977, he was deputy U.S. trade representative, and from 1985 to 1989, he was U.S. trade representative under President Reagan. In 1989, President Bush named him secretary of agriculture. He chaired the Republican National Committee in 1991 and 1992, was counselor to the President for domestic policy in 1992, and most recently, served as deputy chairman to the Bush/Quayle presidential campaign. In what follows, he offers reflections on the Bush presidency.

MR. YEUTTER: In my paper, I will try to provide some insights into the Bush presidency. Because I assumed a number of different roles, I will focus primarily on the big picture. At some point during the last four years, I was immersed in almost everything—from trade and agriculture to politics and economic policy.

I think the world of George Bush. I would not have served in his presidency had I not felt that way. I still feel that way today. I was preparing to leave government service at the end of Ronald Reagan's second term. I had worked for three-and-a-half years and had traveled about two million miles as U.S. trade representative. Then President Bush asked me to take the post of secretary of agriculture. Had he not been George Bush, I would not have done so; I accepted the appointment out of affection for him and a desire to help his administration. There is a financial sacrifice involved in this kind of decision. To become secretary of agriculture, I turned down a position that would have guaranteed me an annual income of $1.5 million. In contrast, the Cabinet post then paid about $100,000 per year. We don't do everything in life for money, however, and in this case, other considerations were paramount.

The defining moment of the Bush administration probably occurred during the 1988 campaign when then-Vice President Bush promised, "Read my lips, no new taxes." It was an important pledge and one that the public took very seriously. It also had a great deal of influence on the outcome of the 1988 election, which he won. I believe he would have been elected even if he had not made that pledge, but certainly it was a powerful political message to deliver at that time.

In 1990, when the White House negotiated the notorious budget agreement that resulted in the breach of the no-new-taxes pledge, it devastated the Bush presidency. Some people in the White House (I was secretary of agriculture at the time) believed that breaking that pledge was not a serious matter because most politicians break their campaign pledges. Why should this one be any different? Clearly, they underestimated the magnitude of the public reaction, particularly from conservatives. Shortly thereafter, I became the Republican national chairman, and I received all of the numerous phone calls and letters that poured into the Republican National Committee asking, "What are those idiots in the White House doing?" Neither the President nor his White House staff fully understood that they would pay a high political price for their actions.

In contrast, there appears to be a different standard for President Clinton's campaign promises, as evidenced by recent *Washington Post* editorials. The *Washington Post* crucified President Bush for breaking his no-new-taxes pledge. Today, after President Clinton has broken innumerable campaign pledges, the line is, "It takes great political courage to break campaign promises and we must commend President Clinton for having the courage to do so." I never saw that newspaper commend President Bush for having the courage to breach his no-new-taxes pledge or other campaign promises.

Although the 1990 budget agreement had some merit and provided some spending disciplines that did not previously exist at the federal level, the breach of that pledge was politically devastating. The spending limits clearly were inadequate, or we would not be facing our current deficit problem. Still, the deficit would be even larger without them. That was the good news. The bad news was that passage and implementation of that agreement inspired Pat Buchanan's 1992 candidacy, which negatively affected George Bush's reelection efforts. It also encouraged Ross Perot's candidacy, which had an even greater negative effect on President Bush's campaign—Perot received 19 percent of the popular vote—and led to Bush's defeat. There were other factors involved, but it is important to remember that once the agreement was signed, Bush assumed a defensive posture politically and stayed there for the remainder of his administration. The Bush administration had to attempt to regain the confidence of conservatives from the signing of the budget agreement through the 1992 Republican convention, something that should have been unnecessary. On the basis of achievements that had taken place early in his administration, the conservative base should have been solidified and available to President Bush throughout 1992. Because it was not available, the President had to expend a great deal of time, energy, effort, and money targeting his conservative base, some of which defected permanently to Ross Perot, at a time when he should have been broadening his political base. In contrast, Governor Clinton effectively appealed to the middle class during 1992, even though his proposals after the election clobbered the middle class. President Bush's inability to broaden his support base brought about his electoral defeat in 1992.

The other element of the Bush presidency that hurt the President a great deal was the recession. While the recession was not nearly as deep this time as many past recessions, Mr. Bush had the misfortune of being president while it occurred. We have had recessions on a cyclical basis for the past 200 years, and I suspect that we will have many more in the next 200 years. Still, you do not want to be president when one of them appears.

The economy remained flat for a long time. When President Bush and others in the administration began speaking of a recovery, no one believed them. It did not feel like a recovery for the large number of people who were unemployed or frightened about losing their jobs. As a consequence, we slid along this recessionary bottom with people saying, "The President is disengaged; he does not know what is happening around the country. We are in the midst of a deep recession and he doesn't know it."

In reality, we had already begun to pull out of that recession, only much more slowly than is usually the case. The United States experienced a 3.8 percent growth rate in the third quarter of 1992, the quarter in which the election was held. Unfortunately, that was not publicized until after the election had ended, so the President received no political benefit. Before the election, the general perception was that we were still in the middle of a recession, even though President Bush was saying, correctly, that it had ended. In fact, the growth rate climbed to 5.7 percent in the last quarter of 1992 before dropping again in the first quarter of 1993. Therefore, although seemingly no one was aware of it, a healthy recovery was underway in the second half of 1992. Had that recovery arrived a quarter or two sooner, I suspect the election returns would have been different.

The credit crunch was one reason for the prolonged recession. For a variety of reasons, banks simply were not lending, particularly to small businesses. Big businesses could still obtain credit through the financial markets, but small businesses had to borrow from banks. From 1990 to 1992, numerous small-business owners told me, "I would like to expand my business, but I can't find credit."

The Bush administration did not address the credit crunch well. I hope that issue is behind us so the Clinton administration will not have to deal with it. Had the credit crunch disappeared earlier, we would have had a more rapid economic recovery and President Bush would probably have been reelected.

The administration responded by telling bank examiners that they were too strict with the bankers and by telling bankers that their conservative lending practices were not contributing to job creation. Basically, the administration spoke to everyone involved, including government lending agencies, in an attempt to convince them to be more active. Whether the Treasury Department and others could have done more, I don't know. Nevertheless, we did not solve the credit crunch.

Paradoxically, winning the Cold War also hurt President Bush politically. From a foreign policy standpoint, that victory was *the* achievement of this century. Its timing hurt the President, however, because it generated a great deal of economic unrest in the after-math. People worried about defense downsizing in many places, California perhaps more than others. In both defense and non-defense industries, companies were laying off workers, and everyone was asking, "Am I next? Will my company start doing it too?"

Interestingly, the greatest level of economic unrest in 1992 occurred among men in the 40-64 age group. Men in this age group worried that they would lose their jobs and never find new ones. They feared that they would be unemployed for the rest of their working lives. That fear was a substantial factor in the 1992 election.

There has also been substantial economic turmoil in other countries, as is reflected by the political concerns that emanated in France with François Mitterrand's recent defeat. Prime Minister

Brian Mulroney of Canada recently indicated that he plans to resign, and Prime Minister Kiichi Miyazawa faces political troubles in Japan, as does Chancellor Kohl in Germany. The entire leadership of the western world is suffering through the Cold War's end. The United States handled the defense downsizing issue well, better than most countries. Still, no one knew it, or at least believed it, last year.

With regard to spending discipline, the Bush administration deserves only average marks, and Congress even worse marks. As a nation, our political leadership has not addressed that issue. I disagree with Ross Perot on many things, but he is correct on the spending issue. Recently, he did a good job of pointing out that President Clinton's administration isn't tackling this issue either. We are currently on the road to having higher taxes and higher spending levels, and we can expect to see little or no improvement in the federal budget deficit over the next four years. There may be a minor improvement in the short run, but it will be accompanied by a significantly higher level of government involvement in our lives.

That trend is not encouraging. President Reagan did a good job in initiating the process of enforcing spending discipline. President Bush did not effectively continue Reagan's efforts, and thus far, the Clinton administration has also accomplished little. That trend must change or we will face an enormous intergenerational fight as the younger generation rebels against the current actions of our generation. We are placing an enormous burden on their shoulders as they move through grade school and high school into positions of political power.

We should begin disciplining entitlement spending. We will never reduce the deficit significantly unless we are willing to cut entitlement programs, which are the sacred cows. No one, Republican or Democrat, has been willing to do so thus far, and it isn't taking place today. President Bush proposed a cap on entitlements in his 1992 budget, but Capitol Hill obviously rejected it. It certainly would have been an excellent step in the right direction.

Ironically, during the last four years, the Bush administration accomplished much more than most people realize, but the media never focused on anything positive related to the President. The media biases in recent years were the worst I have ever seen, as some of the polls clearly indicate. History, too, may well overlook the positive accomplishments and focus on President Bush's mistakes. He will surely receive praise for his foreign policy achievements, but history books will certainly highlight the domestic policy mistakes. His domestic policy achievements will be forgotten or ignored. Had the Democrats not controlled Congress, many more of President Bush's domestic policy proposals would have been enacted into law. Congress, at least in 1992, was determined not to do the President any favors.

Ambassador Carla Hills effectively carried forward the Uruguay Round of the GATT negotiations, the North American Free Trade Agreement (NAFTA), and many bilateral negotiations. We accomplished a great deal on the trade front during the second half of the Reagan administration and through the Bush administration. Many people do not fully comprehend those accomplishments, but we were able to reduce the trade deficit by approximately $100 billion during that eight-year period. We have essentially doubled the level of exports since 1986 and the United States is once again the world's leading exporter. We lead Japan by $100 billion annually in exports, and our international competitiveness is strong. Thus, we have a tremendous record on trade, without which the recent recession would have been far worse.

Our trade position is now worsening somewhat, not because we have lost our international competitiveness, but because no one in the world has any purchasing power. The Western European and Japanese economies are suffering, and those countries are some of our major customers. That downward trend will, of course, change in time as those economies recover.

Both the Reagan and Bush administrations were successful on trade issues. President Bush provided the personal leadership behind NAFTA. We would not have negotiated the North American Free Trade Agreement without that leadership. We also would not have pursued the Enterprise for the Americas Initiative that focused on Latin America had President Bush not taken a personal interest in that area of the world.

On a related issue, Robert Mosbacher, as secretary of commerce, did the country a great favor by holding a series of national technology initiative meetings. At these meetings, business people from around the country shared technology background and valuable information. While these meetings received little publicity, they did an excellent job of addressing needed measures in the technology area and, specifically, export opportunities for our high technology industries. I hope the incoming administration follows Mosbacher's lead. We need to be a high-technology country and expand export opportunities in that area.

We also accomplished a great deal in the agriculture sector during the Bush years. Congress enacted a generally satisfactory farm bill in 1990. Farm legislation is always highly contentious, and the 1990 Farm Bill was no exception. Before we finished, it was about 2,000 pages long—probably 1,500 pages longer than was necessary! Still, the substance of that legislation allowed us to continue efforts to return to a more market-oriented system with less reliance on government subsidies. We still have more government subsidies than we should, in part because we have not yet negotiated agricultural trade reform in the context of the Uruguay Round. We can lower farm subsidies considerably once we convince the rest of the world to commit to similar reforms.

Lamar Alexander did a particularly good job as secretary of education. The reform package that he proposed, which became known as America 2000, was fundamentally strong. President Clinton is now embracing a great deal of its programs, and we hope they will become law. Certainly, better education for our children is a high priority, and through Lamar Alexander, President Bush provided a great deal of leadership in that area. Unfortunately, it did not result in the passage of the necessary legislation.

Lynn Martin, as secretary of labor, undertook the Job Training 2000 program. Again, many of the ideas that President Clinton and his secretary of labor advocate are ideas that surfaced long ago in the Bush administration. For example, through apprenticeship programs we began to focus on better training for young people who do not attend college. Those young people pose the greatest educational challenge we face in the United States today. President Clinton's National Service Initiative, however, targets those people who continue their education in college. It is a good initiative except for its high cost. The priorities are wrong because the emphasis should be on those students who do *not* attend college rather than those who do. At the college level, our educational system is better than that of any other country in the world. We need to concentrate on the youths who do not go to college, many of whom are unproductive and do not fit well in the high-technology world in which they have to work.

Global warming is an area where the Bush administration did what was right and withstood enormous political criticism for doing so. One of President Bush's most courageous domestic policy decisions, which cost him dearly in political terms, was his strong stance in the Global Warming Treaty discussions that took place prior to the Earth Summit in Brazil. U.S. environmental activists wanted to crucify the President and his administration because he would not go as far with that agreement as they wanted. I spent a great deal of personal time on that issue, and I guarantee that we did the right thing. There were innumerable representatives of other countries who, following the conclusion of negotiations, told me, "Thank you for what you did; you took us off the hook. We did not want to sign that treaty in its original form either, but we did not have the political courage to fight back. We are glad you did."

The Global Warming Treaty is an excellent environmental achievement on the part of the Bush administration, without moving too far in the direction of environmental activism. Regrettably, the Clinton administration recently announced that it plans to follow the global warming policy advocated by environmental activists. The American public will pay a price, too great a price in my view, for minimal environmental improvement.

The America the Beautiful Initiative was another excellent environmental accomplishment of the Bush administration. Under that initiative, the Bush administration established a goal of planting a billion trees each year. It is a tremendous program that is just beginning. I hope the Clinton administration gives it the same kind of support that President Bush did.

The Forest Service at the Department of Agriculture played a major role in designing the America the Beautiful Initiative. We have planted a large number of trees in the last couple of years. There will be many more planted if that program continues, and it will be a nice legacy for President Bush.

Given the current widespread focus on health care and Hillary Rodham Clinton's task force, the Bush administration's considerable efforts in that area may not be evident. President Bush's efforts are important in the context of the current debate, however. We had a great deal of discussion on that issue in 1991 and 1992, and decided that the health care challenge was too large and complex to address all at once. We concluded that it would be better to handle the problem incrementally and try to resolve some of the major issues on a bipartisan basis. We wanted to generate broad bipartisan support for those specific issues and thereby gradually narrow the scope of the problem so that it could be dealt with without a gigantic price tag. The Clinton administration has taken the opposite approach by saying, "We will solve the health care problem in one fell swoop."

President Bush submitted four legislative proposals on health care to Congress last year, which comprised the first increments of his health care reform program. The first dealt with administrative reforms, with particular focus on paperwork. Dr. Louis Sullivan, the secretary of Health and Human Services, estimated that we could save about $20 billion annually simply by having uniform administrative procedures. When we presented that idea to Congress, it received widespread bipartisan support, but the Democratic leadership was not about to pass anything for which President Bush might take credit in an election year. For that reason, the proposal went nowhere.

The second proposal encouraged market reforms that would have permitted small businesses to join together in procuring insurance programs for their employees so that economies of scale could be achieved. It would have been valuable to the small-business community of the nation, and it also received bipartisan support.

The third proposal addressed malpractice reform, which appealed to everyone except trial lawyers. This proposal must be passed at some point, because physicians pay enormous sums today for malpractice insurance. That price is ultimately paid by health care consumers.

The fourth piece of legislation made the health care programs of self-employed businesspeople fully tax deductible. Currently, only large, corporate employers are entitled to a full, 100-percent deduction of the premiums they pay for their employees. The self-employed person does not have that same privilege. The tax code discriminates in this area, and we thought that indefensible.

In contrast, the present administration is moving in the opposite direction, with predictable results. The administration's decision to pursue a grandiose program could cost several hundred million dollars per year. President Clinton should have considered the high cost before he embarked on this effort. He has already told people with incomes of $30,000 or above that they will have to pay more in income taxes or energy taxes to fund his other programs. Where, then, do you find the money to fund health care "reforms"? Do you use sin taxes, or do you add a value-added tax to the system? The Clinton administration faces a huge dilemma in deciding how to respond to this question.

The Bush administration was able to pass helpful transportation legislation under Secretary Samuel Skinner's leadership. Ironically, during the campaign, Governor Clinton talked about the need to renovate our infrastructure and increase spending on transportation. The fact that the states were not able to use the money that had already been appropriated under the Bush legislation was unmentioned. Had we increased funding, as Governor Clinton advocated, it simply would have gone unused. The Bush transportation bill received bipartisan support, and currently we are seeing some of its benefits. As a result, more people are working than would otherwise have been the case.

As for crime and drugs, I am not sure what more we should have or could have done. Those issues are difficult to address, and I suspect that history will not grade Bush highly in that area. Perhaps no administration at any level—state, local, or federal— would receive high marks. As a nation, we have not tackled either our crime problem or our drug problem in a satisfactory way. I am not the expert in those fields, but I share the frustration that most Americans have. HUD Secretary Jack Kemp proposed enterprise zones as a creative means for addressing some of the inner-city problems in the country. Unfortunately, he could not move those programs through Congress. We clearly need more creative ideas for addressing crime and drug issues.

A great deal of this challenge relates back to simple, fundamental family values. Vice President Quayle was right when he said that the government cannot solve all of the social problems in this nation. Families have to do it themselves; people have to hold themselves accountable for their own conduct. We must do a better job of helping people to understand this point. During one of the campaign debates, a young man asked the President, "What is the government going to do in these areas?" I wish President Bush had responded, "What are you going to do to help yourself?" We need to look to ourselves instead of depending on the government to find solutions to all of our problems. The government can only do so much in the personal conduct area.

Among President Bush's worthy proposals was his tax reform package, most of which was not enacted into law. Submitted in the 1991 State of the Union message, the package included provisions to enhance capital investment and boost American productivity. The country would be better off today had Congress passed a number of those tax reforms.

Vice President Quayle spoke of civil justice reform. The trial lawyers vigorously attacked the proposals and contributed millions to the Clinton campaign to ensure that there would be no civil-justice reform. Still, it is a good cause, and we need those reforms because we are too litigious a society.

In turning to the administration of government, I would like to make a few comments about the Bush administration. I have worked in Washington for a significant part of the last 20 years. I have served under four presidents—Nixon, Ford, Reagan, and Bush—and I was in Washington many times during the Carter years. As a result, I have observed all of those presidents in action. It is fascinating to watch and compare the management styles of these administrations. I wish I could say there was one that did everything well, but they all have their shortcomings as well as their strong points.

In my view, the quality of the top-level people under President Bush was high. The Bush administration was very talented, and there was a great deal of depth to that talent in a variety of areas. I would be hard-pressed to name another administration that had that level of sheer talent available to it. Much of that was due to President Bush's lengthy record of government service during which he met many people. George Bush knows almost everyone in the political world on a first-name basis, and that helped him attract a great deal of talent to the administration. The present administration has no chance of duplicating the level of talent that was there over the last four years. I do not believe it will even come close. This does not necessarily mean that the Clinton administration will not perform as well; talent is not the only determinant of performance.

With respect to the Bush administration, the high level of performance across the departments is reflected, to a substantial degree, in many of the achievements I just discussed. With one exception, this government was well managed over the last four years.

The one exception was in the regulatory arena where President Reagan, in my view, did a good job of reducing the level of government regulation in people's lives. That situation retrogressed under President Bush, as he will concede. I believe that one of the things the electorate held against him in the campaign was excess regulation. They were hopeful that then-candidate Clinton, who appeared to take a moderate approach to government, might provide some relief in that area. Accordingly, regulation became a negative area for President Bush in the campaign and also in terms of departmental performance.

While we had a well-managed governmental apparatus at the departmental level over the last four years, I do not believe the White House itself was run as well. There were a variety of reasons, including some of the personalities that were involved.

A well-managed White House is important because if the White House isn't running as smoothly or efficiently as it should be, it inevitably returns to haunt the president. In many respects that happened to President Bush, as illustrated by the 1990 Budget Agreement. There were other examples, John Sununu's travel problems being one. All of these problems were distracting, as was the backbiting that occurred among the White House staff, which the *Washington Post* focused on with great relish and through big headlines. Such problems have a tendency to erode the performance of the president.

I wish President Clinton greater success in that regard during his tenure. It is difficult, however, because there are people looking over the shoulders of the White House staff every day, and if they spot something to be critical about, they will be critical.

QUESTION: What are your views about the possibility of a third party in 1996? In 1992, Ross Perot received 19 percent of the vote, and he has not disappeared. Despite what one may think of him personally as a president and of some of his ideas, he appeals to many people at a time when people are becoming dissatisfied with both major parties.

MR. YEUTTER: From my vantage point as chairman of the Republican National Committee, that dissatisfaction was clearly in evidence. As the polls indicate, there has been a great deal of frustration with our party system in this country, and neither party commands much loyalty. In individual elections, people increasingly vote for the candidate rather than the party. That is probably not healthy for our political system, but it is a reality. Both parties need to face that reality and generate greater confidence on the part of the American public.

With respect to Ross Perot, my view is that he will likely run again in 1996. While a great deal could happen before then that might dissuade him from entering the campaign, I believe that he clearly wants to do so. Usually, third-party candidacies dissipate over time. Perot may be unique, however, because we have not had a presidential candidate quite like him before.

A great deal depends on who the Republican candidate is. If the Republican ticket sells well with conservatives, it will pull a large number of votes from Perot and diminish the relevance of his candidacy. Currently, it appears as though there will be many Republican candidates in 1996, so it is difficult to predict who will emerge victorious. Nevertheless, I am positive that Perot would not be a good president.

NARRATOR: Governor Lowell Weicker was at the Miller Center recently and discussed this same question. The audience was made up mostly of students. He predicted that in their lifetime they would see the election of an independent candidate as president.

MR. YEUTTER: Governor Weicker is a little biased because he is now an independent. I would say that the odds of an independent becoming president are well below 50-50, but it could happen sometime. We might see a female president in our lifetimes, too.

QUESTION: Regarding the North American Free Trade Agreement, editorials have argued that if we do not ratify it, we will have much difficulty with Mexico. Could you describe its chances for ratification and what trouble will result if we don't pass it?

MR. YEUTTER: It is vital to America that NAFTA be ratified. It would be a tragic mistake if it were rejected. When I was the U.S. trade representative, I negotiated the U.S.-Canada Free Trade Agreement, the precursor to NAFTA. Fundamentally, we added

Mexico to that agreement and made some additional changes. The U.S.-Canada Agreement has worked exactly the way we predicted. During negotiations, however, people said, "It will be a bad agreement; we will transfer jobs to Canada." Likewise, Canadians worried that their jobs would move to the United States. Some job movement always occurs, but overall, the agreement was a net winner on both sides. Trade between the United States and Canada continues to expand. We are creating jobs on both sides of the border as a result.

These situations encourage demagoguery. Interestingly, in the case of the U.S.-Canada Agreement, the United Auto Workers (UAW) on each side of the border opposed the agreement for exactly opposite reasons. The UAW in Canada argued that Canadian auto jobs would move to the United States. The UAW in the United States opposed the agreement because auto jobs supposedly would move to Canada. One side must be wrong.

Ultimately, Congress passed the agreement by a large margin for good reasons, and it has worked out extremely well. It has its growing pains, and there is still a great deal of opposition in Canada, much more so than in the United States. Nonetheless, it was a beneficial agreement for both countries.

The same is true of NAFTA, when Mexico is added to the picture. The net result will be more jobs in the United States and more jobs in Mexico. There will be better jobs in the United States, which is exactly what we want. There will be some transfer of lower-paying jobs to Mexico. Already, that transfer of jobs is taking place, and it will continue to take place with or without a North American Free Trade Agreement. The agreement may speed the process some because the barriers between the countries will disappear. Nevertheless, while some of these less desirable, labor-intensive, lower-paying jobs move to Mexico, we will be creating more higher-paying, desirable, high-technology jobs in the United States. Politically, the agreement is difficult because people do not look at the average, they look at what they think may happen to them personally. There is a great deal of fear and demagoguery, and as a result, people don't always view it rationally.

If we reject the agreement, it will be devastating for President Salinas. His administration has taken the country a long way. Rejection could easily bring about a leftist government in Mexico to succeed Salinas. Additionally, there is the threat of mass illegal immigration to the United States over time. We would pay a high political price in North America and a high economic price if that agreement were rejected.

QUESTION: You mentioned the problems that President Bush had with conservatives. Do you agree with the opinion that he paid too high a price in his effort to appease the extreme conservatives, thereby losing the moderate conservatives? Also, what do you think the future position of the extreme conservatives vis-à-vis the Republican party will be?

MR. YEUTTER: It is a complicated situation because without a broad political base, elections cannot be won. The Republican party cannot win if it only generates the loyalty of the conservative wing of the American public. It must be able to generate support from moderate, middle-class voters whose political beliefs lie in the middle of the spectrum. Governor Clinton stole a great deal of those votes in 1992, as did Perot, yet Clinton received only 43 percent of the popular vote, which is not a landslide victory. Ordinarily, that is a landslide defeat. The combination of his 43 percent and Perot's 19 percent gave Bush a severe defeat, however.

As a result, by 1996 the Republican party not only has to sustain the loyalty of its conservative base, which I believe it can and will do, but it must also be able to broaden that base to encompass people in the center of the political spectrum. I do not believe there is anything inconsistent in doing that.

In the primaries, the Democratic candidate usually runs to the left to gain nomination and then tries to move back to the center during the general election to capture the moderate votes necessary to win. Similarly, the Republican candidate runs to the right to become nominated before trying to move back to the center to win.

President Bush's problem was that he was still repairing wounds from the Right at the convention in Houston last August. There was not an opportunity to regroup and capture the center. Ultimately, he did not capture the center, and he continued to lose some of the Right to Perot. I suspect that if President Clinton runs again, he will sound fairly conservative in the 1996 campaign, as he did in 1992, even though he is currently governing fairly liberally. Presumably, the Republican candidate will sound quite conservative during the primaries and then less conservative during the general-election campaign.

QUESTION: Our national debt has been increasing at an alarming rate and is the cause for a great deal of concern, especially among people such as Paul Tsongas and Warren Rudman. Could you comment on it?

MR. YEUTTER: It does not look good, and it will be much larger at the end of the Clinton administration if current trends continue. When people in Washington say they will reduce the budget, the cuts are not really cuts. In Washington's jargon, people are really speaking of reducing the rate of spending increases when they refer to cuts. In other words, spending will still increase, just not as dramatically. This occurs often, particularly on Capitol Hill where many people do not want to cut spending.

As a consequence, one must evaluate President Clinton's numbers and the congressional numbers and ask, "Are they really talking about spending less money or are they talking about increasing spending at a lower rate?" Usually, it is the latter; about nine times out of ten they are not talking about decreases. We must start decreasing spending if we are ever going to do anything about the national debt.

Furthermore, everyone says we will save X billion dollars by eliminating government waste, but that is always difficult to pinpoint. Often such talk is a smoke screen for doing nothing. For example, in some of the Clinton campaign materials last year, he had X billion dollars of potential savings on the basis of eliminating waste. He, however, never delineated which programs would be cut. To be credible, one must be more specific. Ultimately, it is a question of effective, solid management in government, just as we expect in the private sector.

The only way to cut government spending is by making major changes in the present entitlement programs. In doing so, however, you confront major interest groups, especially senior citizens. Senior-citizen groups quickly object when anyone talks about cutting their entitlements. Nevertheless, in many cases, low-income, young people are today subsidizing high-income, older people. One must wonder whether that is wise policy.

As another example, one entitlement program in the Department of Agriculture involves food stamps and school-lunch programs. Those programs now account for about 60 percent of the Department of Agriculture budget. Two decades ago, they were a minor percentage. This year, the budget for food programs is about $30 billion, which is a great deal of money. Nevertheless, every time the executive branch goes to Congress to try to cut those programs or cut the daily allowances, it faces a huge political reaction. All of the consumer groups and welfare groups march into Washington saying, "You cannot cut these programs. They need to be increased, not reduced." This example is just one of many.

QUESTION: I hope that Cuba will soon return to the family of nations. What effect will Cuba's sugar production capacity have on their sugar markets?

MR. YEUTTER: Cuba will return sometime, but probably not until Castro leaves the scene. Some of us have been hoping that he might be overthrown, as happened in Eastern Europe and the former Soviet Union. I doubt that will take place. His hold on Cuba is strong, and we may simply have to outlive him. Still, should he depart tomorrow, I would guess it would take Cuba about ten minutes to reject communism. There would be a different government almost instantaneously, and then, things will change.

Cuba's sugar could be allowed into the U.S. market then, but the United States would be under no obligation to permit its entry. That would have to be done on a negotiated basis, and obviously in a democratic society such as ours, U.S. sugar producers would object. As a practical matter, however, we would undoubtedly give Cuba some access to the market.

Furthermore, our sugar program has its own shortcomings. Sugar is one of the most distorted commodities worldwide because of enormous government subsidies, which are funded by taxpayer money. The price for sugar is much higher than it would be without these programs.

If we can achieve global agricultural trade reform, that situation will begin to sort itself out over the next 10 or 12 years. By the time Cuba enters the market, it may not be an issue, and there might be a free and openly competitive sugar market. Cuba would then simply compete.

QUESTION: Does Vice President Quayle have a political future?

MR. YEUTTER: Yes, in my judgment, he does. I believe he was grossly underrated as a vice president and as a political figure. He was battered so unmercifully, and in my judgment, unfairly, by the press that he was never able to recover.

Mr. Quayle is a knowledgeable individual. I worked with him a great deal, and I can tell you that he knew what was taking place around the world, particularly with respect to the economy, as much as anyone else in Washington did. He had a political astuteness that went well beyond that of most people in the Bush administration, and he has good basic political skills.

As Vice President, Mr. Quayle was excellent at political fund-raising. He was our top fund-raiser during my tenure at the Republican National Committee by a substantial margin. I believe he does have a political future, but it may not be in 1996. I would not dismiss him in 1996 yet, but he has a great deal of recovering to do before then, and there is not much time. His future may be in 2000 rather than 1996.

QUESTION: What was the decision-making process in the Bush administration? How did the man in the Oval Office keep his fingers on the pulse of all of the departments and agencies in the administration?

MR. YEUTTER: Most White House staffs operate essentially the same way when making major decisions. Even though many articles have indicated that the Clinton administration is operating differently, it really is doing almost the same thing. The administration has simply changed the names of some of the coordinating and decision-making entities.

Fundamentally, dating back at least to the Nixon years, every administration has an interagency decision-making process in which representatives from the key agencies meet. During most of the Bush years, in most matters of domestic policy, this process took place under the Economic Policy Council, normally chaired by Secretary of the Treasury Nicholas Brady and occasionally by

President Bush. The Economic Policy Council also covered international economic policy. In matters of national security, the process took place under the National Security Council, which was chaired either by the President or by Brent Scowcroft, the national security adviser. When I joined the White House early last year, I assumed management of the interagency process on all but national security issues.

Whether the interagency process works depends heavily on how good the chairperson is. Chairing meetings is an art; some people chair meetings well and are able to encourage discussion and reach a consensus. Some people chair meetings poorly, a consensus is rarely achieved, and little is accomplished.

James Baker chaired the Economic Policy Council when he was secretary of the treasury during the second half of the Reagan years. Secretary Baker is an excellent meeting chairman, and it was one reason why the whole policy apparatus worked exceedingly well in the second Reagan term.

The president too is involved in this process. Typically, if consensus is achieved in the interagency process, the council's recommendation is simply transmitted to the president and he signs off on it. When consensus is not achieved, there will usually be a majority report and a minority report, and the president decides which one to accept. If he is dissatisfied with the outcome of the interagency process, he can send it back and say, "Start over, I don't like your recommendations." Alternatively, he can call a meeting of the interagency group, preside over it, and discuss the matter in greater detail before making his decision.

If it is apparent early on that consensus will not be reached, then sometimes, even before the interagency group makes a recommendation, the president will say, "I'm going to chair this group. We will discuss the issue and then I will make the decision."

QUESTION: Did the President's political advisers, those people looking out for the fortunes of the Republican party and the President himself, help in these considerations of domestic policy?

MR. YEUTTER: Political consultants, who are not in the government, cannot attend interagency meetings; they are precluded from doing so. Still, they can provide input to the administration any time they want. They are well aware of the issues of the day, so they can make their recommendations directly to the president through memos or phone calls, just as James Carville does with President Clinton. Clearly, Mr. Carville gives political advice to President Clinton on a regular basis.

QUESTION: Could you comment on the Gramm-Rudman-Hollings Act and the Budget Agreement?

MR. YEUTTER: Gramm-Rudman was a good law, and I wish it had continued. I believe we, as a nation, made a mistake when we abandoned Gramm-Rudman and shifted to the 1990 Budget Agreement. Gramm-Rudman pinched, which was precisely why Congress wanted to dump it. The Democratic leadership in the Congress particularly did not want its hands tied. Accordingly, they vigorously negotiated in 1990 for a replacement to Gramm-Rudman, and they succeeded.

In exchange for Gramm-Rudman, the budget agreement that emerged had to include some provisions that would help reduce the deficit and some specific budgetary disciplines that did not exist under Gramm-Rudman. Overall, however, it was a poor trade-off because the numbers in Gramm-Rudman were definitive. Unlike the present budget agreement, Gramm-Rudman required Congress to reduce the deficit to a specific number each year. Gramm-Rudman had teeth. The people who like to spend money in Congress were delighted to eliminate some of those teeth, even though they had to accept some other teeth in the exchange. Overall, it was not a good trade-off in my judgment.

QUESTION: With regard to health care reform, I understand that many states are developing their own health care reform plans. Would it be advisable to use one of them as a pilot program instead of having the federal government embrace such a large effort as they are currently doing? Would it be better to take it slowly and do it on a much smaller basis than now?

MR. YEUTTER: One justification for moving incrementally with the Bush administration health reform proposals was for precisely that reason. People are becoming more creative at the state level. They realize that state budgets are becoming as stretched as the federal budget, and they have to find ways to curb costs. That is easier to do closer to home than on some grandiose national scale.

The same argument applies to welfare reform. One of the good things that emerged from the Bush administration was his effort toward welfare reform. We went to the governors and said, "We know welfare is costing you more money than you want to spend, but we do not want to dictate to you what your welfare reforms should be. Why don't you take the lead and tell us what you think will work in your state? If we think it makes sense, we will approve it as an exemption under the federal law. We have some flexibility to do so, and we will let you try it and see whether it works." Many governors are pursuing welfare reform right now, including Tommy Thompson in Wisconsin, Pete Wilson in California, and even James Florio in New Jersey, who ordinarily might not be expected to pursue that kind of program.

There is no reason one could not follow a similar policy in health care reform, or at least in some of its major facets. The national situation is more complicated, of course, and there is the additional problem of people crossing state lines for better care. One can find ways to prevent that problem from occurring, however.

Still, there is a necessary learning curve. We will not solve this problem in a day, and I would like to see some state-level experimentation because there are a number of programs around the country that work well in health care. I serve on the boards of a number of major corporations. Some have now developed health care programs that dramatically cut costs, and they have done it in a variety of ways. Still, they maintain a high level of satisfaction among their employees. These would make an excellent model for American businesses.

Health care reform requires creative solutions. The Clinton administration will rue the day that they assumed this gigantic task. Hillary Rodham Clinton is dedicated to doing the best job she can, but I believe she will discover that an imposed national solution will have a gigantic price tag for American taxpayers.

QUESTION: Are business representatives from companies such as those you mentioned on the task force in Washington?

MR. YEUTTER: No, they were not invited. The health reform task force is fairly broad, but it is also fairly selective.

QUESTION: Could you illustrate how the interagency process works in trade policy, perhaps with the case of Bush's early trade policy toward Japan, after Congress passed the 1988 Omnibus Trade Bill?

MR. YEUTTER: Trade policy works a little differently from other issues, and there is a legislative reason for that difference. Trade is unique in the sense that Congress plays a role in trade agreements that it does not play in most other issues. Congress claims a role in trade policy under the commerce clause of the Constitution. The Senate Finance Committee and the House Ways and Means Committee argue, persuasively in my judgment, that they have a coordinate and cooperative role with the executive branch in the creation and execution of trade policy. Therefore, they more specifically delineate how they believe trade policy should be handled in the United States. There isn't anything like it in any other policy area.

The system that Congress established for trade policy includes the Trade Policy Review Group (TPRG) at the sub-Cabinet level and the Trade Policy Committee (TPC) at the Cabinet level. By law, these entities are chaired respectively by the deputy U.S. trade representative and the U.S. trade representative. During my tenure, we typically resolved around 90 percent of the trade policy issues at the TPRG level, so they never went to a Cabinet group.

When they did go to a Cabinet group, we used the Economic Policy Council, which I discussed earlier, rather than the TPC because the makeup was essentially identical. The process worked well, and most of the remaining decisions were made at that level. Occasionally, one of them was referred to the President. The process was nearly the same under Ambassador Carla Hills.

With respect to trade policy with Japan, that provoked a great deal of debate, and ultimately, the major decisions were referred to the President. The Office of the U.S. Trade Representative did the basic papers, but they were heavily debated and often amended within the Economic Policy Council before going to the President.

CHAPTER 4

THE BUDGET PROCESS*

BRYCE L. HARLOW

NARRATOR: Larry Harlow is vice president and director of legislative affairs for Timmons and Company, Inc., one of the premier government relations consulting firms in Washington. Before joining Timmons and Company, Inc., in 1991, he served for a decade in six senior federal government positions for the Reagan and Bush administrations.

Before working with the Reagan administration, Mr. Harlow directed a governmental relations program for a major trade association in Washington, D.C., and previous to that position, he handled relations with six state legislatures in the Rocky Mountain region for the U.S. Environmental Protection Agency. He also worked in the United States Senate as an aide to one of our Council members, Senator Howard H. Baker.

At the beginning of the Reagan administration Mr. Harlow served as director of the Office of Legislation at the Environmental Protection Agency. Late in 1981 with the confirmation of a new chairman at the Federal Trade Commission, he joined that group and established the first free-standing Office of Congressional Relations in that organization. In the second Reagan term he served as special assistant to the President for legislative affairs again and remained in the Executive Office of the President for President Reagan's entire second term.

Presented in a Forum at the Miller Center of Public Affairs on 2 December 1994.

At the beginning of the Bush administration, Larry Harlow was nominated by the President and confirmed by the Senate as assistant secretary of the treasury for legislative affairs.

I cannot forbear mentioning that perhaps the figure who gave us most heart when we began this oral history program was Larry Harlow's father, Bryce Harlow. Of those people who both participated in and interpreted the presidency, he has been ranked by people of all political persuasions as the ablest and the most clearheaded. I had the privilege of interviewing Bryce Harlow at Harper's Ferry and Crystal City about his experience in the Nixon and Eisenhower administrations.

As for Larry Harlow, his record stands by itself and attests to his strengths and achievements. We are delighted that he could join us to speak about the Bush administration.

MR. HARLOW: I was puzzled by the invitation to speak at the Miller Center. I wondered what on earth a bureaucrat bent and bowed by ten years of service to two administrations could have to say that would be of interest. I realized, however, that I was part of the Bush administration during its first two years when the emphasis was on the budget and on which little has yet been said. Perhaps I can share some experiences from the perspective of someone who was in the trenches for ten years and who saw what went wrong in those first two years of the Bush administration. Those first two years defined the shortcomings of the administration over the entire four-year period.

I would like to step back to 1989 and remind you of the atmosphere that existed at the beginning of the Bush administration. The administration coming into office was to be a kinder, gentler administration. The President and Congress enjoyed their normal six-month honeymoon period. There was a tremendous budget problem, and one priority of the administration and budget officials of the executive branch was to do something about the budget deficit.

President Bush, unlike President Reagan, was a creature of the legislature. He had served in the House and had spent a great deal of his career in Washington. Everyone in Washington expected that there would be a new atmosphere of give-and-take with the wheeling-and-dealing Democratic Congress and that the continued confrontations between Congress and the President that took place during the Reagan administration would subside. For that reason, a great deal of enthusiasm, optimism, and "we can do it" spirit could be found in Washington in early 1989—much as what one sees at the beginning of each administration, such as that of 1993. The new administration of 1989 was a little different, however, because of the seasoning of the individuals involved.

The President had wonderful relationships with Dan Rosten-kowski, one of his best friends and chairman of the Ways and Means Committee, and Tom Foley, the soon-to-be Speaker of the House. Jim Wright was still Speaker at the beginning of the administration. It seemed that the stars had aligned in the correct order so that something could be done once and for all about the budget deficit, which had been the subject by that point of three different so-called summits. Each summit was supposed to be the one that would solve the mess, but the deficit increased after each one because the spending continued.

Ironically, despite these factors, the administration decided at the beginning that the best approach would be to put off coming to final answers on the budget because any of the final answers would involve a repudiation of the campaign pledge "Read my lips, no new taxes." Any attempt to do something serious and final about the deficit would have had to include a sizeable revenue package because the Democrats clearly would have refused to approve the kind of significant budget process reform or entitlement reform necessary for lowering spending to a level where a sizeable deficit reduction over a long period of time could be achieved. Thus, the administration budget officials decided to begin 1989 with the small package. They decided to aim for the big package in 1990.

A problem occurred in 1989, however, when the small package became subsumed by the issue of capital gains, a debate that defined the nature of the relationship between the administration and Congress for the remainder of the Bush term. The Reconcilia-tion Bill resulting from the budget agreement of 1989 began to move through Congress, when it suddenly occurred to some of us at the Treasury Department that we probably had the votes in the Ways and Means Committee to pass one of the President's campaign pledges, a reduction of the capital gains tax. We decided to see if in fact that was the case, and after a week of work, we had enough votes in the Ways and Means Committee to pass the bill reducing the capital gains tax.

We were not able to work out a deal with the committee's chairman, however. The leader of the House of Representatives, Dick Gephardt, was unalterably opposed to it. We then discovered that George Mitchell, who was in his first term as leader of the Senate and who had been cooperative over the years with all of the Reagan and Bush administrations' previous budget reduction efforts, felt that he had been given a commitment from administration budget officials not to raise the issue in 1989. Mitchell thought that the administration had promised not to raise the issue until 1990. No one in the administration can remember making that commitment, and for various reasons, it was decided that the commitment did not exist. As a result, George Mitchell felt betrayed, and his sense of betrayal, founded or unfounded, poisoned the atmosphere from that point forward on any budget or domestic agenda issues that were at issue between the administration and the leader of the U.S. Senate.

A huge fight occurred over the proposed capital gains tax reduction, but it eventually passed in the House. It did not pass the Senate, however, despite the administration's parliamentary advantage against Mitchell in the Senate. The bill was Mitchell's first big test as majority leader. We planned to attach the bill to the debt limit extension so we would have leverage over him. We reasoned that Mitchell would feel pressure to grant the extension in a timely fashion because of the dramatic consequences if he did not. Mitchell, however, refused to allow us to bring it up. He begged the Republicans to back off in the name of good government, and he promised to vote for it later. Knowing that this was George Mitchell's first huge issue out of the box, Bob Dole decided to allow Mitchell some leeway and backed off on the issue. The high-water mark of the capital gains issue came when Dole gave Mitchell control of the floor. At that point George Mitchell found a way to forget his commitment to give Republicans the vote. When the vote finally occurred later in the year, Mitchell filibustered the Republicans. They needed 60 votes to win but only received 51 votes. That battle and the rancor accompanying it set the stage for the huge budget summit in 1990 and the distrust that permeated the process.

In 1989, with the Treasury Department running the legislative efforts, the administration had a wonderfully successful year. Except for the capital gains issue, we had replenished the savings and loans through the Congress and had resolved other budget issues; it seemed as though everything was set for the next year.

In 1990, administration officials tried to engage in summitry again with the leaders of Congress. At first, every member of Congress who was potentially interested in budget issues—and that meant every member of Congress—wanted to sit in on these meetings. As one can imagine, every one of these people wanted to have a say in the final outcome, which is a problem given that the goal of summitry is to reduce the number of participants. Large groups make it difficult to reach a solution to a problem. In 1990, the process began with a large group of participants.

To reduce the number of participants, one must prove that the big group is not efficient. For months, nothing but political posturing happened in these meetings. One side would make an inflammatory remark, and the other side would answer with another inflammatory remark, wink at each other, and return later to the meeting. The administration and Congress developed a tacit understanding that they would not make any progress. This understanding allowed Democratic leaders to get rid of those Democrats they did not want in the meetings and allowed the Republicans in the administration and the Republican leaders in Congress to winnow down the number of Republicans. In short, the reduction process worked, and the groups began to shrink. The problem was that they ultimately shrank too much. The group that finally cut the deal at the end of 1990 was too small. It no longer represented a majority of the rank and file in Congress.

From the administration's standpoint, the small groups posed a different problem. As soon as the groups became small enough for someone to suggest going to the Oval Office for discussions, the administration had a problem.

The administration's handling of the 1990 budget summit was characterized by a series of mistakes, one after another. The first mistake was in allowing any discussions to take place in the Oval Office. In essence, Dick Gephardt, George Mitchell, Leon Panetta (then the budget chairman in the House), and Jim Sasser (budget chairman in the Senate) were allowed to come into the Oval Office and sit down with Richard Darman, Nicholas Brady, John Sununu, and the President to discuss the budget. Once these men were allowed to negotiate in the Oval Office, the President was no longer in a position to disavow whatever was happening. When someone would say that they had heard talk about taxes, he is no longer in a position to say, "That was Brady. I didn't say it." Part of the job of a Cabinet official is to be there, frankly, to take the heat off the president. Once the president's advisers allow the president to be exposed, he can no longer disavow the outcome and thus would have a direct stake in the success of the process. In short, any failure of the process would be viewed as a failure for George Bush.

The other mistake, a huge tactical mistake that characterized the discussions in 1990, was the failure of administration officials to heed, stroke, caress, and keep the Republicans in Congress and across the country informed on what was happening. The best example of this was when administration officials failed to inform Republicans about the decision to renege on President Bush's "no new taxes" pledge. During a meeting in the Oval Office with Democratic leaders, President Bush decided to put out a statement that revenues would be negotiable and put on the table. Either John Sununu or Dick Darman wrote the statement and handed it to Gephardt, who then handed it to Mitchell, who then asked that some changes be made. I cannot recall if any Republican leaders were present at the meeting, but the statement was retyped to reflect the new wording. It was then given to Marlin Fitzwater with instructions to post it on the press bulletin board.

I know this story intimately because of my own involvement. I happened to be in the Senate press gallery at the time, and I noticed that people were suddenly beginning to move around with alacrity and excitement. My pager went off, and I returned a call to the chief of staff for the secretary of the treasury. He said, "I just learned that a statement was put on the press board in the White House about ten minutes ago. Let me read it to you." Included in this statement was the phrase, "including new revenues" to be put on the table. I said, "There goes the pledge! There goes 'no new taxes'!" I told him I would get back to him and then called Fred McClure, the head of White House legislative affairs. I asked McClure if he knew about the statement, and he indicated that he did not. I then read him the portion that I had written down, and he said, "Talk to you later." I then called David Demarest, who was in charge of Public Liaison operations, and told him about the statement. Both he and McClure ran to the press room, fought through the reporters, and read the statement. They were immediately aghast and ran back to their offices and madly began making calls in an attempt to get ahead of the curve, but they were of course unable to do so.

At that point, Republicans on the Hill were being confronted by reporters, saying, "What do you think of this statement?" "What statement?" they asked. "The statement about the taxes that will be on the table. Did they check with you before they put this out?" "No," they answered, and doors were slamming and papers flying. The Democrats, of course, were leaning back in their offices yukking it up at that point, thinking, "Boy, we got them!"

The President was very poorly served that day. When President Bush indicated that he would approve the statement, someone in that room—and that includes my boss, Nick Brady, for whom I have enormous affection and respect, Dick Darman, and John Sununu—should have said, "Mr. President, can I see you alone for a second in the study?" They should have said to him, "We cannot put this out without giving our guys a heads-up so they can cover their tail ends. Give us half an hour." George Bush would have realized they were right and given them a day to review the statement. The alternative was to let Republican party faithfuls around the country feel terribly betrayed by the President's not telling them of this statement. As a result, those Republicans walked away from the President and stayed away.

There is no question that this action had to be taken to get the needed budget deficit reduction. The budget deficit needed to be reduced to drive down interest rates around the world. The United States had to demonstrate to world leaders and its own market that it was serious about deficit reductions so that world leaders would take steps to stabilize interest rates. Moreover, the administration had every reason to believe that the Federal Reserve, upon seeing a sizeable deficit reduction, would lower interest rates in this country. Thus, there were many reasons for the President's decision.

We expected that this concession by the President would make budget negotiations go much more quickly and easily. That did not happen. The Democrats dragged their feet on everything they could throughout the summer. I don't fault the Democrats for this because we let them play this political game every step of the way. The decadent experience at Andrews Air Force Base followed. All of the officers were moved out of their officers' club, and the members of Congress and administration officials moved in. A ten-day discussion resulted in nothing but an agreement to shrink the group more, so the group shrank and went to Tom Foley's office. The group ultimately went to Mitchell's office and all over the Capitol trying to come up with a final agreement.

Before the meetings at Andrews began, Newt Gingrich had already begun to send signals to the White House saying, "You guys had better be careful; the troops are restless; they've never gotten over this 'no new taxes' thing." Gingrich began to show signs that he was not comfortable with what was occurring, especially after the group shrank more. Note what is happening here: Newt Gingrich, the leader of the Republican conservatives in the House of Representatives, was no longer a participant in the negotiations. Though it might have bothered those already in the room, further negotiations should not have proceeded without Gingrich because he was the one who controlled a sizeable block of votes. This litany of tactical mistakes is edifying because it explains why we got into the mess we did.

The next mistake, which was related to the problem of excluding Newt Gingrich, occurred at the conference held by Republicans to talk about the deal that had been reached. At this conference one administration official told all of the Republicans in attendance—that is, every Republican member in the House of Representatives—that the President would be appearing in every congressional district across the country. The official said, "He will be in your district! He will stand on the platform in your district and ask you how you voted on the budget package." Carl Purcell, one of the President's best friends on the Hill, responded, "I have known George Bush longer than you have, and I can tell you right now that he would never go to a district and threaten another Republican with a comment like that." The administration official answered, "Maybe he won't, but I will." Brady and I were sitting there, appalled. Then another administration official got up and answered another member's question about public highway funding by saying, "Obviously, you are unable to understand this matter. Either that, or you don't listen—one of the two." Republican congressmen began shaking their heads and leaving the room. Obviously, the administration was in trouble at this point with respect to getting the necessary number of votes.

It did not need to be that way. Most of those who attended the conference wanted to help George Bush because, frankly, helping George Bush would have helped them. Instead, they came out of the meeting so aggravated and offended by what they thought was the arrogant behavior of the administration that when the vote came up, the Republicans lost, mainly because of the defection of Republican conservatives. They rejected the package in large part to send a signal, not a very pleasant one, to the administration. By voting down the bill, however, the Republicans created a situation in which the administration had to fashion a package to attract more Democratic votes. Thus from the Republican perspective, the package became worse. They knew what was going to happen, but they defeated the bill in part because they were fed up with the way they were being treated by the administration.

This example shows how much of everything going on in Washington is determined by the kinds of human relationships, friendships, and basic rules and protocols that govern day-to-day behavior between humans in every type of relationship across the country.

The bottom line is that the administration became untrustworthy in the eyes of the Republicans on the Hill whose votes we needed. That distrust itself was a result of a number of tactical missteps by the administration during this time. Through their behavior, congressional Republicans communicated their distrust of the administration to the voters, so that the Republican faithful lost their trust in the President too. President Bush was never able to recover this trust even after the Gulf War. As a result, Bill Clinton was elected.

Bill Clinton is now having the same problem. He has lost the trust of the American people. Once you lose that trust, you don't get it back.

QUESTION: Where was the President when all of this was building up? Was he aware of what was happening and did he keep a hand on it?

MR. HARLOW: Yes, to a certain extent. George Bush's focus was not domestic politics. He had very capable budget officials. For example, Richard Darman is one of the smartest people I have ever met. He certainly was capable of handling all of these issues from the spending side. Nick Brady was highly respected on Capitol Hill; those on the Hill trusted him, and I want to emphasize that fact.

Darman may have all of the facts and figures, but Brady had the character they respected. When the deal was going to be cut, they wanted Nick Brady in the room. They knew that if he sat there and nodded, he was reflecting the President's position.

The President was brought up-to-date weekly, or even daily, when things got down to the crunch. The White House normally has weekly legislative leadership meetings in the White House. I don't know if such meetings have occurred as frequently in the Clinton administration, but the Reagan and Bush administrations, as well as the Nixon, Eisenhower, and Ford administrations, held weekly meetings with congressional leaders—either Republican leaders or a bipartisan group of leaders. Obviously, budget issues were always discussed. President Bush had an ability to grasp these things quickly, to understand the basics, and to argue and articulate the issues. He was directly involved in trying to get the budget passed. The problem is that once the president is pulled into this process, as Bush was, his prestige becomes dependent on the outcome. It becomes his loss; it becomes his budget. Bush raised the members of Congress up to his level when he let them into the Oval Office. It is all right to bring them into the Cabinet room for the weekly leadership meetings, but to have them in the Oval Office negotiating the budget is a mistake because it puts the president himself at risk. One wants the secretary of the treasury or the director of OMB to be at risk, but not the president.

QUESTION: How do you feel about tampering with the capital gains tax, both in terms of the importance that was placed on it and in terms of the wisdom of it?

MR. HARLOW: In terms of doing it, I strongly favor a reduction in the capital gains tax—a 50 percent exclusion, such as what we are talking about now. It would unlock resources that have been locked up by people not wanting to pay the tax. The situation is already better now than it was in the period I have just discussed because there is now a 28 percent cap on the capital gains tax. In essence, they lowered the cap by raising all other tax rates. As a result, it is advantageous at the present time for investors to unlock their gains and reinvest them because they only pay a 28 percent tax. The Republicans in general, certainly the House Republicans and most Senate Republicans, continue to feel that further reducing that rate to exclude half of capital gains income would further stimulate the economy by encouraging people to cash in and reinvest.

In terms of the importance placed on it, I thought far too much had been placed on it. It should not become the mantra for the Republican party. As I said before, Republicans won a great victory in the House of Representatives on capital gains, and they had the Democrats in a box in the Senate. They could have made Mitchell and his colleagues blink. All they wanted was an up or down vote on capital gains. The Democrats were filibustering against them, making them come up with 60 votes. Once Republicans succumbed to George Mitchell's good-government argument and backed off on the debt-limit bill, however, Mitchell did exactly what he had been accusing Republicans of doing. As a result, the Republicans could not come up with the necessary 60 votes. When Republicans finally had their vote on capital gains, they only received 51 votes. That is nine votes short of what they needed. Republicans would have had the votes to pass capital gains if it had been a normal vote, not a cloture vote.

I do not think the capital gains issue is the be-all and end-all, frankly. It should not define the Republican party. Nevertheless, at this point, it is unavoidable and will be a key part of the package that comes out of the House and the first one on the desk, if it—again—can get through the Senate.

QUESTION: The Federal Reserve has been increasing interest rates, presumably in an effort to control the expansion of certain resources that would follow an increased reduction in the capital gains tax. Should the Federal Reserve be increasing interest rates?

MR. HARLOW: The Federal Reserve does not need to increase interest rates any more.

QUESTION: Is it acceptable to allow expansion to continue uncontrolled?

MR. HARLOW: Yes, expansion should be permitted to continue. I am not an economist, and I am not going to pretend to be one. I do have certain views on the matter, however, based on my experience heading OMB legislative affairs and Treasury Department legislative affairs and my involvement in many of these issues in the White House, however. I think what the Fed has done is good for the long-term health of the economy, but enough is enough. I think the expansion should be allowed to grow more than it has and that unlocking these resources—these capital gains—for reinvestment in long-term investments is, again, good for the country. I would like to see people free their capital gains and reinvest them in other long-term investments in the country. I am not talking about freeing the capital gains so people will run out and spend them. I do not think people would do that. They will find other ways to invest them, perhaps in new types of investments or new types of growth investment in the country. This will serve the country's best interests in the long term. I do not have hard empirical data with me to back up my statements, but that is what I think will happen.

QUESTION: What do you foresee for the Gingrich-Archer formulated budget and its passage?

MR. HARLOW: They are in desperate shape, frankly. Right now, pandemonium reigns behind closed doors in Washington, and I have to race back to be trampled by it this afternoon. The Republicans now are like the dog that caught the car, particularly in the budget sense. Remember, the House Republicans have never been responsible for preparing a House budget resolution because they have never had control of the House since the establishment of that process. The Senate Republicans are in slightly better condition because Pete Domenici has done it before. They have been responsible for Senate budget resolutions, but they have never been responsible for one in conjunction with the House.

In the budget process, the president submits a budget. It is then immediately discarded, and the House and the Senate each write their own budget. They come together, and a conference committee writes a congressional budget resolution that is the budget of the United States of America. That version will include the so-called reconciliation instructions, which will include spending cuts and tax increases reconciled to the various committees of Congress and the various subject areas. The Republican staff in the House right now is just a shadow of the staff that the Democrats have had for years. I'm not saying this as a partisan. I think any objective observer would look at the way the staffs have been treated in the House of Representatives, particularly over the last 15 to 20 years, and see it as a travesty of justice and probably a usurpation of representative democracy. For instance, on Energy and Commerce, there are 140 Democratic staff members and 17 Republicans. How is that reflective of the 62 percent Democrat majority in the House of Representatives? It isn't! As a result of these staff imbalances that have built up over a long period of time, one Republican staffer was trying to do what five or six would be doing on the Democrat side. It is remarkable that the Republican staffers have done as good a job as they have.

The result is that now the Republican have control, they are incredibly unprepared because they have been browbeaten and hammered down for the last 20 years. Because the new Congress does not come in until January, that same small Republican staff is trying to develop a budget that was supposed to have been started in August. When the six Republicans on the House Budget Committee suddenly found themselves in charge of the process, they thought, "Maybe we had better call the Commerce and Treasury departments and find out what they want." To their surprise, they found that the Treasury Department and the Commerce Department are run by Democrats who do not feel like cooperating one bit with the Republicans.

The Republicans are in a difficult situation because of procedural problems that they face and because there is not enough money to do what they want to do. So Newt Gingrich makes comments like, "Let's put Social Security off budget." Budget officials hear that and have to be helped off the floor because if Social Security is put off budget, about a quarter or a third of the federal revenues would be wiped out, which would be disastrous. That is what they are going through. Archer will be able to move quickly in some areas and not so quickly in others.

Other factors are at work here as well. The Republicans in the House of Representatives have made a commitment to have a so-called open house. Thus, 75 percent of the bills to be considered on the House floor will be considered under a so-called open rule. That practice used to be the norm in the House of Representatives but was abandoned during the tenure of Tip O'Neill and Jim Wright, so that almost everything that came to the floor in the

House was written with precise rules by the Democrats to keep Republicans from being able to offer amendments on certain subjects. In short, the Democrats controlled the entire process.

Republicans have said that this approach is wrong and that they will do something about it. They intend to live up to their promise. Now when bills come to the floor, people can come up with many ways to amend them. That has happened for some time in the Senate, which does not have germaneness rules. Senators can add an amendment on any topic to a bill. The Senate process is based on unanimous consent so agreement is necessary for everything. It has not always happened that way in the House, however. Think about that when a capital gains bill moves to the floor. Democrats will be able to come in from left field and get amendments included on all types of other controversial issues with only the flimsiest thread of germaneness. The new open-house rule will make it very difficult for the Republicans to live up to their pledge of passing bills in the first 100 days of the new Congress.

What people will probably see is Newt Gingrich having absolute control over the Republicans in the House, where they will back him on every parliamentary ruling from the chair. He will have to have that kind of control or there will be pandemonium on the House floor because the Democrats will jump up and do whatever they want and try to embarrass the Republicans and have a good old time on C-SPAN. The parliamentarian or Gingrich will make rulings from the chair. They will try to be concise with them, but sometimes they will be provocative and controversial. When that happens, the Democrats will appeal the ruling of the chair, and it will come down to the majority ruling. Rules are only good as long as votes are available to back them up. Rules votes will take up a great deal of time on the House floor because of these types of problems.

No one part of the Republican pledge can be looked at alone. There will be a domino effect. Dominoes could be stretched from here to Washington that have to be tipped over regarding the changes now occurring in that town.

QUESTION: What do you think about the chances of cutting government—for example, by reducing the sizes of staffs and committees?

MR. HARLOW: The chances are very good. There will be a reduction in the size of staff in the House of Representatives. The committee staffs will be reduced by one-third, and there will be fewer committees. There will have to be fewer committees because one of the rule changes the Republicans will make is to end the practice of proxy voting, where an absentee committee member gives the chairman or someone else a proxy, and that person votes it the way he or she wants. Republicans are going to stop that practice because it has led to the proliferation of committees and subcommittees. Requiring the presence of committee members to vote would limit the number of committees on which a single representative could serve because he or she can only be in one place at a time. Thus, the elimination of proxy voting will necessarily shrink the number of committees in the House.

It will also shrink the size of committees. Committees have become huge. The Appropriations Committee in the House now has 62 members, but it will soon shrink to about 52 members once proxy voting is eliminated.

The Republicans will not do anything as dramatic as the things they maintained immediately after the election. They will not eliminate the Energy and Commerce Committee, for instance. They will do some fine-tuning. The Republican strategy is based upon the thesis that real changes can only be made right after an election that has changed control of Congress and before the new party is in power. Otherwise, the vested interests and the bureaucracies link up with their appropriate committees, and the iron triangle is back in place. The members on the committees do not want to give up their relationships to the bureaucracies or to the vested interests that are now special interests that have become beholden to them.

NARRATOR: Could you refresh everyone's minds about iron triangles?

MR. HARLOW: The reference I used for iron triangles—and there are others—is the relationship between a powerful committee in Congress, the bureaucracy that is beholden to that committee, and the special interests regulated by the bureaucracy that try to influence the committee that writes the laws regulating the bureaucracy. The committees are responsive to the constituencies because the constituencies help committee members get elected; thus it is a representative democracy in that sense. Once iron triangles are in place, it is extremely difficult to break them up.

QUESTION: With respect to Bush's unexpected decision to make revenues negotiable, you mentioned that a half hour's or day's warning might have allowed the administration's spokesmen or spinners to make the decision palatable to other Republicans. Would you comment further on this issue?

MR. HARLOW: Ideally, this development would have occurred over a period of months, during which the administration would have successfully demonstrated its commitment to deficit reductions by its many concrete spending cut proposals and other revenue-raising ideas—such as user fees, which were rejected by the Democrats. The administration had made such proposals, but the public was not aware of them. Everything happened behind closed doors.

One of the lessons to Republicans of this process is that such closed-door methods are not in their interest. In 1990, the budget negotiations were moved to Andrews Air Force Base to cloak them in secrecy and to keep any knowledge of the negotiations from becoming public so that we could work in a trustful atmosphere. The Democrats, of course, leaked a great deal of information. I am not saying this as a partisan, but the next day we could read in the newspaper what had been said the day before. Republicans were playing by the rules and not talking to the media. Members of the media today tell me, "You guys were being played; you were such idiots. Every day after the negotiations, people for Mitchell and Sasser on the Budget Committee would brief us and put their spin on what was taking place. You guys didn't do a thing, did you?" We replied that we thought we were playing by the rules. They called us babes in the woods! We should have played the game and set the situation up much better than we did.

In August of 1989, about four of us went to Easton, Maryland, to sit down with Secretary Brady in the basement of an old home of his and review the situation. We concluded that given the need to send a message to the markets and do something about international interest rates we needed a budget deal, and we would have to put revenues on the table if we wanted a budget deal. There was no way around it.

Once that decision was made, two questions remained: When should we do it, and How should we do it? With respect to the first question of timing, we wanted to do it as far in front of the next election as possible. To do it immediately before the next election would have been self-immolation. We thought it would be wise to put revenues on the table as quickly as possible. I think the timing issue was properly decided. It was the second question of how to do it that was botched.

The failure to handle this issue properly is an indication of what was structurally wrong inside the White House. To put it bluntly, everything was at the top, and not enough bait was put in the White House apparatus to convince people to do the job they had been hired to do. The administration should have had Demarest handle public relations with its constituencies and Fred McClure handle the Congress, but that was not done. If it had been handled in that manner, the umbrage and feeling of betrayal might have been greatly diminished. In answer to your question then, all of the blame cannot be laid on that one instant, but this episode is a great example and probably the crowning moment of our tactical mismanagement of the entire 1990 budget process.

NARRATOR: Other presidents have put foreign policy first. For example, Nixon chose his foreign policy team before he did anything else, and people are still puzzled that his domestic and economic team was as weak as it was. In the Bush administration, some people have said that Nick Brady lacked the necessary knowledge for the position he held. Was the media attention focused on Brady and the others one reason the economic policy suffered?

MR. HARLOW: There was a conscious decision in the administration to resolve what it saw as the outstanding domestic issues in the first two years before turning to foreign policy in the second two years. The situation in Kuwait changed that to a certain degree. Iraq's invasion of Kuwait took place in August 1990, just before we went into the summit conference at Andrews Air Force Base. Incidentally, Brady joined the budget summit conference at Andrews straight off a plane on which he had flown around the world raising money from the allies for the war effort. Though successful, Brady came into the budget summit without any sleep, exhausted.

To be fair in assessing the administration's handling of the budget process, people should consider that the President was in a box once Kuwait occurred. If the budget process did not reach a successful conclusion, a sequester of incredible proportions would have resulted. This sequester would have sent a terrible message to our putative allies about our commitment in this area and about our ability to get our act together. Once the United States was headed toward war with Iraq—actually, once the United States even began efforts to get Saddam Hussein out of Kuwait—we could not allow the message to be sent that the United States was going to cut defense forces by one-third. The sequester would have been of monumental proportions. For instance, the United States might not have had the ability to airlift troops and supplies on a moment's notice. Finishing the budget quickly became a priority. The necessity for haste has to be factored into any analysis of the budget situation.

Regarding your point about domestic versus foreign policy, remember that Nixon was successful domestically during the first two years of his administration. He was very successful in creating the Environmental Protection Agency and various other domestic initiatives. He had problems, obviously, with some Supreme Court nominations, as George Bush did with John Tower's nomination as secretary of defense, but by and large Nixon was in a strong position. George Bush was not necessarily in a strong position heading into the last two years of his term. His weakened position is a reflection of the problems the United States had domestically those first two years. The first year was very successful, but the second year was a disaster.

QUESTION: If Newt Gingrich appoints the chairmen of those various committees, will he be overreaching his power or authority? Will he create disharmony in the Republican party as a result?

MR. HARLOW: The Speaker of the House is elected by members of the majority party. If he is overreaching himself, they will not elect him as Speaker. It is important to remember that over half of the Republican party in the House of Representatives are either freshmen or just finishing their first terms and beginning their second terms. Thus, over half of the Republican members are new-comers. As a bloc, they are the ones that have the votes on Newt Gingrich. Gingrich has to be responsive to these new people. My friend who is participating in the transition meetings said, "I'm going into these meetings all the time with these little kids, and then I realize they are congressmen!" That is what Gingrich is dealing with.

I think Gingrich will be elected by acclamation. He is considered the prophet by Republicans in the House. He was the only one who believed the Republicans could win a majority.

Last night I was with Newt at a dinner where he gave an extemporaneous speech, which is the way he delivers all of his speeches. He does not use notes or read from text. Gingrich is very intelligent, and he retains everything. He is doing a great job of handling this transition. The proof will be seen on opening day. The House will have the longest opening day in the history of the Republic. It will enact all of the rule changes Republicans promised. On that day, Congress will pass legislation to guarantee an open House and a reduction in the size of its committees. It will mark a dramatic change in the operations of the House. I think as time passes, the American people will like Newt Gingrich more and more. Frankly, I am making comments that I would not have made four years ago about Newt Gingrich, but I am completely sold on him now. He has done a fabulous job, and he is doing a better job every day in the way he is handling himself.

NARRATOR: We have been very fortunate to have Larry Harlow with us today. He knows government well and has made a significant contribution to our Bush oral history series.

III

FORMING AN
ADMINISTRATION

CHAPTER 5

PERSONNEL AND THE SELECTION PROCESS*

CHASE UNTERMEYER

NARRATOR: When did your association with George Bush begin?

MR. UNTERMEYER: My association with George Bush began in September 1966. He was a candidate for Congress from the new seventh district of Texas, which is where I lived. It is the affluent western half of Harris county, encompassing essentially the affluent suburbs of Houston. I had met him—just a handshake—at a Young Republican gathering in October 1963 when he was Republican county chairman.

NARRATOR: Did you have some immediate or initial impressions of Bush? Did those perceptions continue, or did they change over time? If so, in what ways?

MR. UNTERMEYER: I do believe that the George Bush with whom I just had lunch is very much the same man I met in 1966 when I did some campaign work for him. He is very much the same in terms of his personality, warmth, and interest and liking for other people, which never varied no matter what heights he attained.

---

*Transcript from a telephone interview conducted at the Miller Center of Public Affairs on 15 February 1994.

NARRATOR: How was the Bush administration organized for selecting personnel and what were his general priorities in the organization of personnel?   What is your evaluation of his approach?

MR. UNTERMEYER: As the director of presidential personnel under Bush, much of what I will say relates to the people chosen to do the governing. We begin, of course, with the Cabinet. I have often said that George Bush was probably the first president since Franklin Roosevelt, if not earlier, who was personally acquainted with every member of his Cabinet before he named them to office. They were people he had known and with whom he had worked for many years. As a result, he had preexisting personal relationships of one sort or another, varying from close and intimate friendships, as with Jim Baker and Nicholas Brady, to lesser friendships, as with such colleagues from the Reagan administration as Elizabeth Dole and Dick Darman. The current administration illustrates what happens when a president selects people based on their resume and what other people say about them. When the president himself is not personally acquainted with these appointees, it is unfortunately too late to begin to get to know that person after he or she has already been appointed to the Cabinet.

Bush's White House staff reflects his conclusions as to how government should be run. After seeing the Reagan White House close up and the Nixon-Ford White House from a distance, President Bush did not want to have a White House staff that was in any way superior to the Cabinet in rank or attitude. He believed that the White House staff should be just that—a staff. Staff members should not be governors in an actual sense. The White House staff is active in policy-making, and many presidential decisions go into the formulation of actions taken on a departmental level. There were, nevertheless, no cases in which a member of the White House staff was a boss of the Cabinet secretary, unlike the way I sense that arrangements were in the Nixon, Ford, and Reagan administrations.

NARRATOR: Was the White House staff large enough to handle its tasks?

MR. UNTERMEYER: I don't think the President's personnel staff was large enough at the crucial time to do all of the needed interviewing, but that is the only part of the staff about which I can speak.

NARRATOR: Was the White House staff efficient, or did problems arise?

MR. UNTERMEYER: President Bush acted swiftly on anything that reached his in-box, and I think that is the hallmark of efficiency. As long as I have known him, he has been the sort of man who wants to clear his desk before he goes home, and he sometimes clears his desk several times during the day. That little factor is of an inestimable value and is appreciated by staffers seeking guidance and direction. Some people let decisions wait on their desks, a situation that creates frustration. Often a leader—and George Bush may well have been one of them—will sit on a particular matter if he doesn't think the time is right. That situation is different, however, from cases in which people just cannot bring themselves to make a decision or get distracted by other things and let the paperwork mount up. Thus, the fact that concerns were addressed promptly—generally never more than overnight or over the weekend—added a great stimulus of efficiency to the system.

NARRATOR: Was the rest of the Bush administration effective and helpful from the standpoint of your responsibilities?

MR. UNTERMEYER: Yes, I have no general complaints. The position with which I related most directly and frequently was the White House counsel.

Incidentally, I think the fact that the White House counsel himself was deeply involved in policy-making did not work so well in the Bush White House. I hasten to say that this is no criticism of Boyden Gray's having a role. I simply believe, having lived through a White House, that the White House counsel, *qua* counsel, should be the staff's lawyer and as such should be responsible for moving the legal paperwork. I have no objection to an attorney who is held in high esteem by the president, as Boyden Gray was, having a major policy-making role. In such an instance, however, the person should have a different title with responsibilities other than running the White House legal staff. Most of what the White House legal staff does is pure paperwork of a boring nature. For example, the crux of my relationship with the White House counsel's office was ensuring that they were moving expeditiously to check the financial papers of a prospective nominee. This type of work is all important, of course, but often it would be delayed while the legal staff of Boyden Gray's office, which was composed of many former Supreme Court clerks, pursued work on clean air, civil rights, or Supreme Court nominations. The fact that this office had an important policy-making role meant that routine paperwork was delayed while attention was given to these other more glamorous and important things. I recommended to Bill Clinton's transition leaders, namely Warren Christopher and Vernon Jordan, that the White House counsel should be the staff lawyer and that if the president wanted to have someone be a policy counselor, then that is a different sort of role altogether. They did not necessarily take my advice, but I think that is what happened—the current counsel, Bernie Nussbaum, is the White House lawyer and does not have a policy-making role.

NARRATOR: Would problems of that type, as you or others have identified them, be discussed with President Bush, or is that something people would not bring to him?

MR. UNTERMEYER: I certainly did not. Stories circulated during 1989 about Bush's slow pace in making his appointments. Note that this story has yet to die with Bill Clinton—there is great public awareness of the many vacancies in his administration. When those stories were hot and heavy in 1989 and the President began to worry about why it was taking so long to get people in place, I discussed the reasons with Chief of Staff John Sununu. He was the proper problem solver who knew what needed to be done.

NARRATOR: To turn to the president's end of this situation, one of the criticisms of President Carter was that he never took command of the bureaucracy. He never had a sufficient channel to the bureaucracy so that his ideals and his policy views could filter down through the bureaucracy, rather than being limited to the White House. Did President Bush function well in that regard?

MR. UNTERMEYER: Without apologizing for Jimmy Carter, having command of the bureaucracy in a functional military sense of the word is a problem for any president. President Bush certainly believed in the chain of command, which was exemplified by his conduct in the Gulf War. The reason he had confidence and trust in the chain of command is that he had first-rate people immediately below him. He could expect that they would be able to take command of the bureaucracy. It is beyond my ability to comment on how each and every Cabinet secretary controlled their respective agencies. Presidents often wake up, read the *Washington Post,* and discover something happening within the bureaucracy that is a total surprise, as much as it would be to any other reader in the country. That is what happens in large organizations. In fact, that situation occasionally arises in a corporation, which is *the* model of efficiency vis-à-vis the federal government.

NARRATOR: Was President Bush quite effective in dealing with personnel matters within the government? Was it a matter that interested him, and one that you and he occasionally discussed or could discuss if a need for such a discussion arose?

MR. UNTERMEYER: He took direct interest in the highest-level appointments, namely, those for the Cabinet and Supreme Court. Occasionally, certain other appointments were of interest for policy reasons or because of friends whom he wanted to see in those positions. The vast majority of the appointments were delegated to the chief of staff [John Sununu] and me and then brought to President Bush for final approval through an ordered process.

NARRATOR: I suppose one of the big items that occupied people was the Sununu question. Looking back, all things considered, did Mr. Bush handle that situation as well as he possibly could?

MR. UNTERMEYER: I look on John Sununu as chief of staff differently from many people because he and I had an excellent relationship. Of all of the things I have read about John Sununu—that he was arrogant, snarling, and impetuous—I never saw these qualities in him. It could have just been me, but I also suspect it was true of other people as well. Reputations are sometimes built on echoes of echoes. In the case of John Sununu, my favorable outlook could well be because the one and only thing about which I ever came to see him was personnel. As a former governor who had to make appointments, Sununu had personal knowledge of that system. Like many people who had that responsibility, he also realized the problems of the job, so he was happy that my staff and I dealt with the nitty-gritty. Still, he could not escape the phone calls from senators and others who would protest some personnel decisions. I found it regrettable that John Sununu was lost to President Bush because of the episodes we all read about in the newspaper. I contend that John Sununu was exactly the right sort of person to be chief of staff.

He had two unique qualifications required of a proper chief of staff. One was unwavering loyalty to the President; he had the President's interests at heart. Second, he had direct executive experience as a state governor. While there is a vast difference in scale between New Hampshire and the United States, I contend that responsibility and stress are as great for the governor of a small state as for the President of the United States. As such, John Sununu brought a very valuable experience to his position of chief of staff. Notwithstanding these qualities, John Sununu's problems led to the tragedy of his resignation.

NARRATOR: Was there a list of "dos and don'ts" set out at the beginning of the administration regarding use of airplanes and other such matters, or did President Bush not micromanage those aspects?

MR. UNTERMEYER: No, I don't think President Bush did. Boyden Gray would have been the one responsible for those ethical issues.

During 1988, the Dukakis campaign made much of what they called the "sleaze factor" of the Reagan administration—a highly overdone allegation that anyone who had an unfavorable story written about them in the *Washington Post* was ipso facto guilty of high crimes and misdemeanors. That was the pertinent campaign issue during part of 1988. Candidate Bush issued a promise that if elected, he would in effect have a special counsel for ethics. Essentially, it would be a second White House counsel—one to deal with all matters of ethics, including the clearance of prospective nominees, and the other to be concerned with the ordinary daily workings of the White House and the administration. I think Boyden Gray was party to that proposal, but I am not sure how involved he was because Craig Fuller may have been the principal author. Sometime on or before the election, Boyden said that the responsibility of the White House counsel should not be divided, that *he* should be the person responsible for ethical matters as well as the other business of government. That is how the situation was in actuality. This structure led to the problem I mentioned earlier, when the burden gets to be too great and ethical matters are often seen as a lesser responsibility as a result.

NARRATOR: One of the questions that arises with regard to any president is his response to crisis. Did you have any personal experience in observing President Bush operate in a crisis other than the Gulf War?

MR. UNTERMEYER: The most famous instance I did observe prior to the Gulf War was the day President Reagan was shot in March 1981. This situation certainly gave me the most vivid exposure I had ever seen of him in a period of crisis. He was extraordinarily calm, even to the point of serenity, which is an important factor for anyone dealing with crisis matters. He handled matters with dispassion and then made decisions on what to do. He was not all aflutter, which was the condition back in the White House situation room that same day.

NARRATOR: One puzzle about the Bush presidency was how relaxed and calm his attitude seemed to be during press conferences at the beginning of his administration, in contrast to some other presidents. Then the media seemed to go after him and perhaps took advantage of that open format and his honesty. Did you have a chance to observe any of the press conferences?

MR. UNTERMEYER: None, other than being close to a television monitor at the time of a press conference. I led a very insular existence confined to presidential personnel because that job is so all-consuming and confining. When I read that Bill Clinton's first personnel director, Bruce Lindsey, was traveling on Air Force One with the President, I could not imagine—even to this day—why he would ever want to leave the security and sanctity of that office. Not only did he leave the office, he also went directly to face all of the state party chairmen, campaign leaders, congressmen, and senators who were trying to beat down his door to get jobs for their associates. I was very happy to be basically isolated and insulated with people and paper.

NARRATOR: I remember how you have said on another occasion that the number of days that you had gotten out of Washington were very few.

MR. UNTERMEYER: In fact, the only time I ever set foot on Air Force One was the day of the 1993 inauguration. (Officially, that plane was no longer Air Force One.) I had a chance to see what the airplane was like on a trip to Houston with the Bushes, but I had never before wanted to be on board.

NARRATOR: Many of the Ford people claimed there were fewer scandals in that administration than in many of the preceding administrations, and except for a few incidences that were widely publicized, I don't remember many scandals in the Bush administration.

MR. UNTERMEYER: I certainly do believe that few personnel scandals was a hallmark of the Bush administration, and indeed, he said emphatically that he wanted a scandal-free term. We were also careful. New people yielded a surprise or two during the background investigation process, but I must say that of all of the problems President Bush carried into his 1992 reelection campaign, administration "sleaze" was not one of them.

President Reagan was accused of sleaze, which is just a political term that unfortunately stuck. I don't think the Reagan administration was in any way sleazy, but George Bush's opponents in 1992 did not have occasion to use that term at all. A person who can speak authoritatively on this matter is Stephen Potts, who was head of the Office of Government Ethics. I have heard him say publicly that he felt the Bush administration was quite scandal-free, largely because of the care that went into the recruitment and especially the vetting of prospective appointees. Stephen Potts is now in Washington practicing law.

NARRATOR: One thing that has puzzled many people is George Bush's behavior during the campaign. Some theories have been circulated about it but nothing firm has emerged. For example, Charley Bartlett has told me several times that he just didn't recognize George Bush during the pre-campaign and the campaign itself. Some people have said that they had known George Bush for 40 years, but the real George Bush or the Bush they knew was not the same person who delayed actively participating in the campaign and was lethargic in the debates later in the campaign. Some people suggest a medical reason and other people suggest other reasons. What are your thoughts on that perception?

MR. UNTERMEYER: I don't believe that decisions made and not made in 1992 were the result of President Bush's state of health. I believe that what drove many of the decisions, such as the campaign team's late start and various other matters of tactics, was the fact that George Bush was the one primarily calling the shots; that is, as a man who had been counted out politically several times throughout his career, always rising back higher than he started, he believed in his own good judgment. Unfortunately, his judgment failed him in 1992, because starting the campaign so late and not having a more politically acute campaign team hurt him. I don't think, however, that those things defeated him. He was defeated because of the economy and H. Ross Perot. In fact, those two factors were more important than Bill Clinton. George Bush's loss was not caused by the fact that the campaign began six weeks later than it might have.

I also believe that George Bush was hurt politically in 1992 by three deaths that occurred earlier in his administration. Lee Atwater, had he lived, would have been precisely the kind of campaign strategist and tactician that was needed, especially against a couple of characters like Clinton and Perot. Two other men much closer to George Bush had also died—men who would have given him the direct, wise, and shrewd counseling he needed. One was Malcolm Baldrige, secretary of commerce (1981-87) and head of Bush's campaign in the 1980 Connecticut presidential primary. Baldrige died in 1987 and would likely have had a major role in the Bush administration had he lived. The other was Dean Burch, former campaign manager for Barry Goldwater, chairman of the Republican National Committee, chairman of the Federal Communications Commission, and at the time of his death in 1991, president of Intelsat. He had exactly the same kind of standing with

George Bush—a direct, personal friendship and a political kinship going back many years, far longer than Lee Atwater. Unfortunately, the departure of all three of these men meant that there was no real sage who was able to help Bush. James Baker, who was certainly of that same class in terms of his personal relationship to George Bush and his own political background, was totally consumed by the job of secretary of state. I don't blame him for not wanting to give that job up to go back to the White House. I don't blame him for using his brain cells to try to figure out the Israeli-Palestinian problem as opposed to what to do for the first, second, and third debates. That problem often occurs after winning campaigns: Your best campaign people are given government jobs where they are either forbidden by law from being politically active or are too absorbed by government issues, hindering their service to you in the next campaign.

NARRATOR: Speaking of Baker, did you play a role in the President's selection of such a compatible and congenial national security team as Cheney, Scowcroft, Baker, and Powell?

MR. UNTERMEYER: I wish I could claim a hand in that selection, but it was definitely in the hands of George Bush. That is a good example of what I said at the outset about President Bush's having long-standing personal relations with his top people. I think his method of selecting top people will be a legacy of the Bush administration. The fact that the administration has been deemed a political failure by some has not taken away from the quality of people who served in it. I predict that the next Republican president, especially if he or she is wise, will find and take advantage of a great talent pool of people who had served in the Bush administration in all levels and all departments, a great training ground for people in the business of government. That talent pool is an enormous asset for the Republican party. The lack of such a pool is a great deficit for the Democratic party. I hope I was shrewd enough to predict at your conference table in April 1989 that now that the Democrats are back in power, they are having a great problem finding the quality of people necessary to fill high-ranking positions because they have been out of office for so long.

NARRATOR: How do you view the environment created by the far Right and President Bush's mode of dealing with it, evident at the convention but also evident in the constant barrage of criticism that after Ronald Reagan, President Bush was not a true Republican? Was he effective in meeting that criticism or question? Or could he have done anything about it?

MR. UNTERMEYER: In the whole political history of George Bush, one of the most fascinating aspects was his relationship with "movement" conservatives, or the far Right—whichever you want to call them. We are talking about a group of people who are far more varied than I am making them appear, so I hope to be forgiven. Nevertheless, they are a group who had never supported him politically or felt comfortable with him until 1988. He himself found it uncomfortable to think back to his experience as the Harris County Republican chairman in 1963, when people passed out literature that essentially said: George Bush is the son of Prescott Bush, who was a partner at Brown Brothers Harriman & Co., a firm that included Averell Harriman, who was advising Franklin Roosevelt at Yalta; therefore, George Bush is part of the group that gave away Eastern Europe.

Other less logical and less astute claims also circulated. Bush therefore not only felt uncomfortable with this group of people, but he also felt that reaching out to them was fruitless and in vain. Essentially, that was his conviction throughout his first term as vice president. I am convinced that Lee Atwater's enormous contribution to making George Bush president was getting Bush to realize around 1985 that he needed to begin courting the conservative element, not only because of its importance for any nominee, but because he could at least blunt their opposition to him. The success of that strategy was evident in the 1988 primaries. The fact that Pat Buchanan arose in 1992 is a result of the lack of Lee Atwater. I am not sure what Lee would have done or said to George Bush prior to 1992 that would have staved off that split in Republican ranks, but I have every faith that he would have known how to deal with it.

The great irony is that in looking at the 1992 voting results, the Christian Right was the most loyal element to George Bush. States like Mississippi and Utah were the ones most strongly in his corner when the election was over. The thing I say to my friends who talk about "the horror" of the Houston convention and the power of the Republican Right is that such an intensely loyal, highly disciplined group of people should not be pulled from your voting majority. Statements about "Houston" are, in fact, the standard ones used by the people who feel as though the Republican party is somehow weakened by having that element.

NARRATOR: How did you and the President divide the work on appointing sub-Cabinet people? That group of people seems to have been very strong when they emerged. Larry Eagleburger is an example.

MR. UNTERMEYER: Larry Eagleburger is a special case. In many ways the position of deputy secretary of state is not really a sub-Cabinet position. Jim Baker probably thought of Larry Eagleburger for that job, but when he mentioned his name to George Bush, Bush immediately knew that suggestion was a great idea. He knew Eagleburger and had great confidence in him. The vast amount of sub-Cabinet positions, however, were filled by people George Bush had never known and may not have seen except in a large gathering.

Essentially, either the Cabinet members or the White House chooses the people who serve at the sub-Cabinet level. Neither method works very well, however. When the White House chooses all of the sub-Cabinet members, the Cabinet officers feel that their deputies are aliens within their group. No one wants to feel like an outsider, as that feeling can easily hinder one's effectiveness at work.

If on the other hand the Cabinet secretary chooses sub-Cabinet members, he or she may choose fine and able people, but those appointees may not have any prior loyalty to the president. Thus, when times get bad, they may be the ones to make the anonymous quotations heard at cocktail parties or leak telephone conversations over the wire to newspapers that often prove to be embarrassing to the administration. These leaks are more likely to happen when appointees feel that they received their positions because of their own brilliance rather than their prior loyalty to the president.

George Bush tried to find the middle road, which is conceptually the right way to do the job, but this path had its own problems. The middle road requires cooperation between a Cabinet secretary and the White House personnel office. The personnel office was supposedly the keeper of the flame of the Bush campaign and would be promoting candidates who had worked in it. Meanwhile, Cabinet secretaries might be promoting hot shots from Wall Street who didn't have a direct connection with the president. This meant making compromises. That is essentially how selections were made, and there were only a few occasions when disagreements went even as far up as chief of staff, let alone to the Oval Office. The primary exceptions I remember were in the two biggest departments—namely, Defense and Health and Human Services. The Cabinet secretaries there had strong ideas about the kind of people they wanted, most of whom had no prior Bush political credentials. Some of Secretary Cheney's people at Defense had worked in Republican politics, mainly on Capitol Hill, but not in President Bush's campaigns.

NARRATOR: There are many talented people in the Defense Department and other places. I recently spoke to Alberto Coll, who was deputy assistant secretary of defense in the Bush administration. He and others had careers on Capitol Hill and in the universities.

MR. UNTERMEYER: This subject could be an entirely separate lecture. I do not know how one would solve the appointment problem other than the way Bill Clinton has—that is, on paper. What I understand about his operation is that he insists that he review the sub-Cabinet appointments. I think that is tremendous. After all, the Constitution doesn't mention assistants to the president for personnel; it doesn't even mention a chief of staff. If the president becomes involved in those sub-Cabinet cases, that is what he was expected to do by the Framers. But what I understand is happening now is that no action is taken on those personnel folders, so they remain on the Oval Office desk. If that is the case, then you have the worst possible system where names languish in the Oval Office, and then everyone is unhappy when no decision is made.

NARRATOR: I gather without even asking that you think history will be kind to George Bush.

MR. UNTERMEYER: Yes, but I cannot get away from the fact that he received only 37.4 percent of the vote in 1992. I wish I could change that result. If it were not for Ross Perot, Bush would have been reelected—not by a landslide, but reelected. At least then he wouldn't have that blemish on his career. Some people say that Ronald Reagan was a success ipso facto because he got reelected. Although the significance of his reelection cannot be denied, that criterion is too trivial because Reagan's success had to do with what he did in office. I wish that in 1992 we had the economy of 1984. A better economy would have done a great deal to give George Bush the same kind of luster as Reagan. Notwithstanding the fact that he lost, the things he accomplished, the people he put into high-ranking positions, and the standards he embraced gave the United States a sound, good government, which is basically what the people wanted.

George Bush is criticized for not having a vision or a policy. I think that surprises him as much as anyone because it was not clear that this was what the American people wanted. What he represented was a continuation of the philosophy of the Reagan years. While some people say he betrayed Reagan because he raised taxes or kept regulating, they overlook the fact that Ronald Reagan also raised taxes and allowed regulations to continue. They overlook the fact that George Bush was President of the United States because he had been Ronald Reagan's vice president. If he had articulated a different vision for his administration, perhaps people would have had grounds to say he was trying to betray Reagan. I find it sad that some people try to drive a wedge between the Reagan and Bush administrations.

NARRATOR: Thank you for another informative discussion.

IV

THE MAKING
OF FOREIGN POLICY

CHAPTER 6

THE MAKING OF FOREIGN POLICY IN THE BUSH ADMINISTRATION[*]

JOHN R. BOLTON

NARRATOR: On 9 January 1995, John R. Bolton was appointed president of the National Policy Forum by Republican National Committee Chairman Haley Barbour. Mr. Bolton graduated Phi Beta Kappa from Yale College before receiving his J.D. degree from Yale Law School, where he was also an editor of the *Yale Law Journal*. From 1989 to 1993 he was assistant secretary of state for international organization affairs for the Bush administration. He was responsible for managing the formulation and implementation of U.S. policy within the United Nations system, including U.S. policy during the Gulf crisis from 1990 to 1991. Mr. Bolton reported directly to the secretary of state and supervised the approximately 450 employees involved in U.S. missions around the world, including New York, Geneva, Vienna, Rome, Paris, Montreal, and Nairobi.

Prior to this time, Mr. Bolton served from 1988 to 1989 in the Reagan administration as assistant attorney general of the civil division, the Department of Justice's largest litigating division, and before that as assistant attorney general in the Office of Legislative Affairs (1985-1988). Mr. Bolton also acted in the capacity of general counsel of the U.S. Agency for International Development

---

[*]*Presented in a Forum at the Miller Center of Public Affairs on 25 May 1995.*

(USAID) from 1981 to 1982 and was assistant administrator for Policy and Program Coordination from 1982 to 1983.

When not in public service, Mr. Bolton has been both associate and then partner in the law firm of Covington & Burling. Just prior to his appointment as president of the National Policy Forum, he was president of Bolton Associates, an international legal and consulting firm that worked with both American corporations and foreign bodies and firms with activities in the United States. He was also a senior fellow with the Manhattan Institute from January 1993 to January 1994.

We look forward to hearing about the strategic maneuvers and policies that were pursued by Lawrence Eagleburger and others in the Bush administration, as well as the role of the United Nations and the United States in this period of U.S. history.

MR. BOLTON: I knew President Bush only slightly at the beginning of his administration, although I had served in the Reagan administration. My involvement in the Bush administration came from knowing Jim Baker for many years. My friends who were running Baker's campaign for attorney general of Texas in 1978, a campaign Baker lost, approached me with several legal issues regarding campaign statutes in Texas. I had just finished the case *Buckley v. Valeo*, which resulted in a Supreme Court decision in 1976 invalidating several aspects of the post-Watergate federal campaign finance laws, and my friends probably thought that my knowledge of federal election laws translated into knowledge about Texas election laws as well. As it turned out, I did not know much about Texas election laws, but I did meet Jim Baker during that time.

When Bush became president, one of the central elements of his personnel policy as articulated by Chase Untermeyer, Bush's director of presidential personnel, was a clear decision not to retain any presidential appointees from the Reagan administration in the positions that they held at the time. That decision was based on a historical assessment of other presidential transitions, particularly the transition between Coolidge and Hoover, which was the last orderly Republican-to-Republican transition. Other same-party transitions occurred, but they were of a different character—for example, Roosevelt-Truman, which was not a transition by election; Kennedy-Johnson, which again was not by election; and Nixon-Ford.

In short, the 1928 transition from Coolidge to Hoover was the last normal same-party transition, and the Bush team felt that Hoover was disadvantaged by his decision (or lack of decision) to retain key presidential appointments from the earlier administration. As a result, Untermeyer's rule of thumb was basically "new faces in old places and old faces in new places," meaning that anyone from the Reagan administration remaining in the Bush administration would be placed in a different job.

This decision also had its roots in Bush's determination to centralize personnel decision making in the White House. How presidents choose to select their personnel varies from president to president. In Bush's case, however (this method was used by Reagan as well), he felt that Carter's decision to permit his appointed Cabinet secretaries to choose their own top staffs was a mistake because it resulted in a weakening of White House control over the executive branch. For this reason my own appointment was somewhat awkward, as I received my job through Jim Baker rather than George Bush. In fact, I remember meeting Chase Untermeyer at the White House after the inauguration, and he told me that he was very glad I was going to be assistant secretary for international organization affairs but then asked me to give him a copy of my resume for his files. He was very gracious about it. Nevertheless, I was an anomaly in the Bush decision-making process, and I think my appointment is reflective of the overall relationship between Bush and Baker and how they functioned together in foreign policy decision making.

In fact, it is impossible to understand foreign policy-making during the Bush years without understanding or at least recognizing the personal relationship between George Bush and Jim Baker. Indeed, I cannot think of a closer relationship between a president and a Cabinet official since John F. Kennedy and his brother, Robert F. Kennedy. In many ways, Baker and Bush were like brothers. They did not always see things the same way. They had their disagreements, and they too experienced some ego jostling back and forth. The relationship between the two men was nevertheless very close, and one cannot understand the decision making of the Bush administration without giving consideration to that fact. Bush and Baker's relationship is a clear example of how the boxes and lines on an organizational chart do not always accurately depict reality; in this case, the personal relationship explained much more about decision making than any organizational chart.

For example, the role of the NSC staff was much reduced from what it had been in other administrations, though I am not speaking of Brent Scowcroft's role as Bush's national security adviser because he also had a key personal relationship that had a profound impact on policy. What I mean is that in terms of day-to-day work at the State Department, little attention was paid to the NSC staff. The President deliberately chose to place decisions about national security issues in the hands of his closest advisers, including Defense Secretary Dick Cheney. There just was not much time for bureaucratic infighting. Moreover, this determination to have the principals work on a very personal basis is one factor that characterized the successes of the Bush administration. The Bush administration's personal approach to decision making was typified by the weekly breakfast, sometimes a lunch, attended by Jim Baker, Dick Cheney, and Brent Scowcroft. If at any point an issue had trouble being resolved through the regular bureaucratic process—for example, through interdepartmental meetings or the deputies committee system—the staff knew that the weekly breakfast group could be decisive when the staff could not. If one wanted to roll the Department of Defense, the best way to do it would be to tell Baker. That way he could get it done at the lunch or breakfast, and then the staff would not have to worry about that issue anymore. This method may not be an elegant way to make decisions, but it was extraordinarily effective and quick. In addition, the breakfast group recognized that if they could not make a decision about an issue, it obviously had to go to the President with no need for further delay.

Perhaps both as a result and an advantage of this informality, it was better able to respond to crises than the more bureaucratic approach. The players had a sense that decisions should be made and not just massaged endlessly. One of the best examples of the effectiveness of the Bush decision-making process and an effectively functioning bureaucratic system was the Gulf crisis, which was the central defining event of the entire Bush presidency. During this crisis, an incredible number of decisions had to be made through the deputies committee mechanism in a relatively short period of time. In the meantime, big decisions were made in the Oval Office with Baker, Cheney, Scowcroft, John Sununu when he was chief of staff, and frequently the Joint Chiefs of Staff chairman, Colin Powell.

I sometimes went with Baker to the White House and sat in the office of the President's secretary while this little group of people made some of the critical decisions. Occasionally, Baker would come out and ask something like, "What's the procedure in the Security Council? We want to do *X*." I would explain the procedure to him, and he would go back in. Meanwhile, I would wait and wonder about the outcome of the meeting and try to figure out what I was supposed to do next. This example is typical of the way in which President Bush liked to proceed. Endless mechanisms of decision making did not interest him, though the deputies committee meeting was an effective way for many of the lower-level decisions to be made.

From the State Department's point of view, the deputies committee is sort of a misnomer. The lead person was Bob Kimmitt, who was the undersecretary for political affairs at the Department of State and who, given the manner in which Bush and Baker ran the State Department, became a kind of crisis manager on a day-to-day basis. The process also used technology to its best advantage. For example, the key elements involved in the Gulf crisis were the NSC, which was represented typically by Robert Gates, the office of the secretary of defense, the Joint Chiefs of Staff, the CIA, the State Department, occasionally the Justice Department, and others. Instead of everyone leaving their respective offices, however, teleconferences were held. Signals had to be scrambled to ensure the confidentiality of the meetings, but a great deal of time was saved by holding meetings in this fashion. The staff could still fax information to each other and communicate with people in the other affected agencies, but it would be through cameras and television screens. Charts could be displayed in the same manner. Many hours were saved during the Gulf crisis by not having to travel to the White House and go through the formalities of security procedures. As a consequence, much decision making occurred below the level of the principals.

One thing about the Gulf crisis that is absolutely critical to understand was the basic insignificance of Congress in decision making until the end when the dilemma of whether or not to use force arose. The timing of Saddam Hussein's invasion of Kuwait had a great deal to do with Congress's small role. The invasion took place at the beginning of Congress's August recess, and few things take precedence in the life of a congressman over getting out of town for that month before Labor Day. Another contributing factor was that in the early days of the crisis, especially after the initial invasion, not everyone understood that the United States was at the edge of a truly historic series of events. Having been out of the country for the first two or three days of the crisis, I had a perspective on the situation that perhaps others did not have. Not realizing what the significance of the invasion would be, congressmen and much of the press were not in Washington that August. The absence of the press was not a bad situation either. We were spared the kind of interactive conversation that can get in the way of policy and process. No questions like "How do you think they are doing today in the administration?" with a response being "Another big mistake today" were heard.

Congressional hearings were not held in the first month either. Politically, most members of Congress probably did not know how the Gulf crisis would turn out. They did not know its impact in their constituencies or what the long-term implications would be. They were just as happy being in their districts as the Bush administration was to have them out of town. Consequently, when the congressmen returned to Washington after Labor Day, they saw a series of diplomatic and military events unfolding under a single leadership. Moreover, the political fear of getting involved in the middle of this unfolding decision-making process and the fact that they had not been centrally involved at the beginning kept them on the margins until the end of the crisis—and I do mean the end. Congress remained on the sidelines through the U.N. Security Council's authorization to use force in November, the military activity itself, and even during the three or four months after the military side of the crisis had ended and the humanitarian relief effort for the Kurds in the north had begun.

This absence of Congress as a political and policy-making force during most of the crisis allowed the executive branch to make decisions with a minimum of outside political interference. Whether good or bad, it certainly made decision making much easier, compared to circumstances in which the administration continually had to take Congress into account. For instance, in Cambodia, which measured about 0.5 on a scale from 0 to 100 of vital U.S. interests, the staff was constantly worried about Congress and what it was saying about policies, yet in the great political scheme of things, Cambodia just did not register with the American electorate at all. Because of the high level of congressional involvement on a relatively minor issue, the administration was always thinking about how the next hearing on Capitol Hill would look.

Few concerns occurred along these lines during the Gulf crisis. I testified perhaps twice on the Gulf crisis between August 1990 and January 1991. From my point of view these hearings were perfunctory because I was able to tailor my answers very carefully, thus leaving us maximum flexibility in subsequent policy-making. By the end of the hearing, my testimony made no difference in the decision making of the Bush administration regarding the Gulf crisis.

The one key point on which Congress did have a role in the Gulf crisis was on the authorization for the use of force. That factor was certainly taken into account in much of the administration's decision making, but it did not impinge upon it on a day-to-day basis. The reason for lack of interference goes back to August as well. Immediately after the invasion, as senators and representatives were leaving Washington, they were asked by the press whether at some point they would agree to a congressional authorization of the use of force if Saddam Hussein did not withdraw. This next remark is of a partisan nature, but I remember the Democrats distinctly replying to the questions of the press by saying that they might consider voting to authorize the use of force if the Security Council voted to, which in early August 1990 sounded like, "We'll vote to authorize the use of force when the cow jumps over the moon." It was a safe comment for them to make. At that point, although no decision had been made to seek an authorization to use force from the Security Council, it seemed very unlikely that the United States would be able to get the necessary nine votes in the Security Council because no one knew what would happen in August 1990.

Between the time of the invasion, the Security Council's vote, and the series of resolutions that were adopted either unanimously or with only one or two negative votes or abstentions, much of the diplomacy was directed toward the possibility that the administration would have to seek a resolution from the Security Council authorizing the use of force. Although I do not think a lack of authorization from the Security Council would have stopped Bush from making the decisions he did, it did play a role in the administration's strategy toward Congress. The administration debated about whether it should first approach Congress or the Security Council. If Congress was approached first for an authorization to use force, that strategy would allow the Bush administration to tell the countries on the Security Council that there was no question as to what U.S. policy was.

Over the course of the administration's discussion with Security Council members, Canada was the only country I remember that asked the administration whether it would get congressional approval to use force. Like most Americans, most of the world does not understand the separation of powers in the U.S. political system. With the exception of Canada, the other countries on the Security Council looked to the executive branch to tell them what American policy was without considering the role of Congress. As a result, the administration did not deliberate long about whether it should approach Congress first or the Security Council first. Clearly, it would go to the Security Council first and Congress second.

In obtaining the Security Council vote, important questions had to be asked and answered beginning in early August: When was the last time the Security Council voted to authorize force in international conflict? The answer was Korea. How did they do it? The answer was that the Soviets were boycotting the Security Council and thus did not veto it. Could the United States get the same kind of command structure in 1990 that it used to get—for example, the resolutions in the summer of 1950 when an expressed blessing was given to the American command structure in Korea? The answer was no. Then how was the administration going to get what it wanted? The questions continued in this fashion. This thought process was an enormous intellectual exercise quite apart from the diplomatic efforts.

Having served in the Justice Department under Edwin Meese, I am constitutionally an originalist in thinking, so of course we reviewed the records of the drafting of the U.N. Charter to find out what people really thought. We reviewed the records of countries such as Finland that were on the Security Council, which went through its own internal national debate about whether they were going to vote to authorize force. Eventually, of course, the Security Council adopted Resolution 678 in November. At that point, my involvement essentially ended, leaving the White House and others to contemplate how to get the authorization to use force from Congress. The significance of that order of events (going to the Security Council first and Congress second) was that Bush orchestrated an international coalition to support the use of force before he could get Congress to do it. The way I always like to put it is that he got Finland to vote in favor of authorizing force before most of the Democrats.

President Bush's reputation as an incredibly hands-on president in foreign policy and as one who was very knowledgeable about all of the details of the situation in general is deserved. More than one time I remember having a conversation about the Security Council with Baker in his office, and he would have the President on the phone talking about Security Council procedure. Baker would hold the phone away from his ear so I could hear the President's conversation and write down what I was supposed to do. When I say a hands-on approach, I mean a hands-on approach.

At the same time, however, the way President Bush handled the Gulf crisis can be contrasted to the President's decision-making style in other foreign policy situations and in domestic policy in general. The President was extremely detached from domestic policy, a situation not without political implications. For example, that detachment eventually caused the political difficulties that led to his failure to get reelected in 1992. When I say detached, I do not mean uninterested. I mean only that he handled domestic policies in a clinically detached way.

An example of the President's detachment was his inability to convey to U.N. Secretary General Boutros Boutros-Ghali his irritation with the different domestic constituencies that had an interest in the Yugoslav crisis. Secretary General Boutros-Ghali had come to see the President during one of Boutros-Ghali's annual meetings in Washington in the spring of 1992. Bush tried to explain to Boutros-Ghali the domestic context in which the United States had to make its policy toward the Balkans. The President referred to the summer of 1991, when the administration had issued a statement expressing the hope that if Yugoslavia were to dissolve, that it would do so peacefully. This statement was issued in the shadow of Slovenia's impending declaration of independence, but the President had not mentioned that aspect in his statement, thus irritating the Slovenian Americans. He then proceeded to tell the secretary general about what the administration did (or did not do) to irritate the Croatian-Americans. Then one cannot forget the Serbian-Americans, who were irritated by the administration's condemnation of Serbian aggression. Secretary Baker looked at the President quizzically as the President proceeded to tell Boutros-Ghali something else the administration had done to irritate another domestic American constituency. Right then, Secretary Baker, who rarely interrupted the President in these meetings, said, "Mr. Secretary General, I just want to emphasize what the President said about how irritated the Slovenian-Americans, Croatian-Americans, and Serbian-Americans are." Instinctively, Baker knew that these aspects were all flags. The President was just very detached in a way he was not during the Gulf crisis.

Between the end of the Gulf crisis and the election, the administration just drifted along; there was no crisp end to it. As a result, President Bush did not get reelected in November 1992. Curiously, however, the loss in 1992 also freed the President from these pesky domestic political considerations. He got back to foreign policy.

I would like to discuss the decision concerning Somalia because a lot that has been written about that decision is wrong. In deciding whether the United States should intervene in Somalia, a great deal of discussion took place concerning what the United States could and should do and what the United Nations could do to address the humanitarian emergency that everyone perceived there. The administration, particularly in the career ranks, was divided as to what to do. This division had much to do with what happened during the opening year of the Clinton administration; that is, the Bush administration was divided in terms of its reliance on multilateral institutions for the implementation of U.S. foreign policy.

The context of the Somalia operation in 1992 was that the U.N. peacekeeping force sent to prevent fighting among the various Somali factions from resulting in or exacerbating the humanitarian situation had essentially failed. The U.N. peacekeeping force had been minimally deployed; it had been ineffective and had not done anything to bring the situation under control politically or militarily. Consequently, the debate within the administration in the fall of 1992 basically came down to three options. One was a huge U.N. presence in Somalia that would simply by its size, if nothing else, stabilize the situation and permit the distribution of humanitarian assistance. The second option was a kind of increased U.N. presence—that is, one larger than the one that was there during most of 1992 but nothing like the size of the one proposed in the first option. The third option was a relatively massive U.S. intervention.

The people who proposed the large U.N. presence were basically senior career foreign service officers who had no U.N. experience. Their proposal is significant because they like many other Americans misunderstood what the United Nations could do. They looked at the Gulf crisis, the successful election in Namibia, the efforts in Central America to end the two civil wars and establish democratic systems there, and the role of the United Nations in Afghanistan. They concluded that the United Nations could do much more than it ultimately was able to do.

The intermediate view, the increased U.N. presence, was the one I advocated. The third view, which was massive U.S. intervention, was the Pentagon view, contrary to what one might normally expect. At the State Department, the general belief was that the Pentagon thought the United Nations was not capable of meeting this humanitarian emergency. The Pentagon's point of reference was northern Iraq after the war, which was in fact a correct assessment of the United Nations not being able to handle the situation without U.S. military involvement. Nevertheless, many in the administration thought it was kind of cynical for the Department of Defense to say, "You want to stop starvation in Somalia? Then we will put in 30,000 American troops and that will square the situation away very easily; no problem. It would only take a division and we will probably only be there about six months." No one in the State Department thought that Bush would agree to that plan. I thought it was more likely he was going to take the first option—the massive U.N. presence, which I thought was a mistake.

On the day before Thanksgiving in 1992, two-and-a-half weeks after the election, a meeting was held at the White House that included the President, Baker (who was then chief of staff), Larry Eagleburger, Scowcroft, Cheney, and Powell. We expected them to emerge with something between a massive U.N. presence and the increased U.N. presence that I had been proposing. Seeing that it was the day before Thanksgiving and Bush had already lost the election, I fully expected to be able to leave early to see my family.

Instead, Eagleburger came from the meeting to say that we were going to New York to talk to Boutros-Ghali. The President had decided on American intervention. President Bush did not believe that either U.N. option would be effective in alleviating the humanitarian tragedy. Given the proven effectiveness of the U.S. military operation in the Kurdish situation in northern Iraq, the President figured that U.S. intervention was the only operational decision that could really have an impact in the short period of time needed to avert what was then feared to be massive starvation and loss of life.

Note that the Somalia concern was not about complicating things for the incoming Clinton administration. President Bush did not say that he wanted to stick them with Somalia. Neither was Somalia about ending the Bush administration with a flourish. There was no discussion about how the Bush administration would be remembered. The decision to intervene in Somalia involved instead a very plain discussion about which option operationally would be the most effective. From the beginning, the administration intended the operation to be limited in humanitarian terms to opening channels of relief, though this proposal did not necessarily mean that American forces would be out by 20 January. We did, however, tell the Clinton people that if they did not want to continue the operation, everyone could be out by the 19th so that the decks would be clear for their own decision making. They said no, however, and that we should proceed. They would work at whatever point the Bush administration left off.

I wrote an article on this subject in the January/February 1994 issue of *Foreign Affairs*. My piece was more of a critique on the Clinton administration, but in it, I make the point that Somalia, the last major foreign policy decision made by the Bush administration, was characterized by the same kind of decision-making approach that characterized the Gulf War. Indeed, both are successful examples of Bush's personal style of decision making.

One aspect of the Bush presidency was that Bush did more than any other president to communicate with foreign leaders by telephone. He used this method because he knew so many of them, but also because it was another aspect of his style. The career people at the State Department used to call him the "Mad Dialer" because of his many and frequent calls to foreign leaders. In fact, it is pretty clear that Vernon Walters, the U.S. ambassador to

Germany at the time, resigned because he was tired of hearing from the German foreign ministry that the President had been on the phone to Chancellor Helmut Kohl again and that they had agreed on some other aspect of German-American bilateral relations. One extreme example involved the President calling French President Francois Mitterrand to discuss a draft of the sanctions resolution. Mitterrand might say that he did not like some aspect of it, and he and the President would discuss possible changes. As I say, he really understood the process and did it hands-on. Nevertheless, many people were frustrated in having to adjust to that kind of personal style.

President Bush's personal style of diplomacy raises larger questions about the future of diplomacy in general. Technology is going to change the entire way that diplomacy is conducted. Moreover, it is going to change very quickly in the sense that capital-to-capital discussions will be more important than ambassadors. President Bush's style was probably ahead of his time, but even so, people must recognize that they live in different times. This is not the 18th century when Benjamin Franklin would be sent to Paris with three or four pages of instructions, knowing that the next boat would not get to him for three months.

Jim Baker's role in the Middle East negotiations highlights a different aspect of high-level diplomacy. It did not matter how many ambassadors the United States had in the Middle East or how many area experts it had. The discussions that led to the opening of the talks in Madrid and virtually every other important aspect of the Middle East peace process after the Gulf War personally involved Baker (in conjunction with the President). The point to note is that such high-level, personal involvement and direct discussions take place outside of the traditional diplomatic channels.

NARRATOR: Some people have said that the Somalia action was a response to the intense media coverage of the crisis. Is this statement accurate? Was the fact that Bush was clinically aware but not emotionally caught up in domestic politics as Baker was a factor in making them such a good team? Finally, would you comment on Congress's attempts to intermingle domestic issues with foreign policy?

MR. BOLTON: Without question the media's coverage of Somalia brought it to a higher level of attention. Nevertheless—and this distinction is significant—the level of coverage did not dictate the policy. It made the Somalia issue more important, but it did not dictate U.S. actions there. The proof of the media's influence lies in the fact that an almost equally devastating situation in humanitarian terms was evolving unnoticed next door to Somalia in the Sudan. Similarly, Liberia's civil war had been going on for two-and-a-half years before that point, yet Liberia did not receive the kind of attention that was devoted to Somalia.

In terms of the Bush-Baker team, I think even Baker was much more concerned with foreign policy than domestic. He did, however, react to domestic concerns better and was more aware of them than Bush was. I remember that as early as January 1992 when we flew to Mexico City to sign the El Salvador agreement, Baker was already worried about what the President's political situation was. That was eleven months before the election, when most people would have said that although Bush's campaign was not where it should be politically, it was not really in bad shape either. Baker, however, knew then. He kept saying that the situation had all of the earmarks of Carter's situation in January 1980.

As for congressional involvement, I am not sure that the bills that are now working their way through Congress are really fundamentally different from previous congressional efforts to control foreign policy. For example, in the Iran-contra debates, the critical statutory provision in the Central American context was the Boland Amendment, which in its various permutations and most significant provision, limited the number of American military advisers in El Salvador to 31. With respect to congressional interference in executive branch foreign policy decision making, that limitation is pretty significant. The Boland Amendment is a worse case of congressional interference than some of the things on the current bill being debated in Congress. The tug-of-war between the President and Congress is an ongoing problem, but I do not think it is any worse today than it has previously been. In fact, I think it confirms what I have been saying, which is that the Bush administration was mercifully free of this problem on many of these issues.

QUESTION: Shouldn't an automatic time limit be placed on any U.N. Security Council resolutions? It seems that resolutions should expire at a given time unless renewed. I am thinking in particular of the aftermath of the Gulf War. Many resolutions still in existence never seem to end.

MR. BOLTON: I do not think that time limits and sunset provisions on Security Council resolutions are good ideas. The reason is that if no time limit exists either in the Charter or the resolutions themselves, then changing a resolution requires another vote by the Security Council, which is in U.S. interests because the United States can always veto a resolution to change an existing one. My view is that anything that preserves and strengthens the veto is a good thing for the United States. For example, Resolution 687, which is the cease-fire resolution against Iraq, will stay forever. The sanctions will remain in place. All of the provisions regarding weapons of mass destruction will remain in place. Everything will remain unless another Security Council resolution changes it. Think about how the French, the Russians in particular, and the British to a lesser extent might want to weaken the sanctions in order to buy oil but cannot because they know they have to get the United States to agree to do it. On the other hand, if a sunset provision were included, they would be in Baghdad today buying the oil.

Your point is valid in that some resolutions are universally agreed to be outdated. For example, the resolution granting the right of return to Palestinian refugees in the wake of the partition of the Palestinian mandate theoretically still exists. Theoretically, all of those people in refugee camps in the occupied territories have a right to return to what is now pre-1967 green-line territory in Israel, which the Israelis would never allow. Nevertheless, that resolution still exists, and all the United States can do is hope people forget about it.

QUESTION: In her memoirs, Margaret Thatcher commented on a meeting that she had with George Bush after the invasion in August 1990. What do you think Margaret Thatcher's memoirs will reveal about what she said to George Bush and how influential she was in goading and pushing Bush?

MR. BOLTON: The chapter to which you refer in her book *The Downing Street Years* (1993) is titled, "No Time to go Wobbly." She never says in that chapter, however, that she told Bush, "Now

George, this is no time to go wobbly on us," which was a remarkable piece of restraint given that, as I understand it, she really did make that comment. Bush's relationship with Thatcher was not anything like that of Thatcher and Reagan by any stretch of the imagination, but her saying that she was no longer going to tolerate Bush's handling of the situation thus far probably caused him to think of an answer.

COMMENT: In 1988 when George Bush accepted the nomination, he was a fireball, ready and full of energy. This image is in sharp contrast to the George Bush seen at the 1992 convention. There, he gave the impression that he did not have the energy, did not really want to be reelected, and was not pushing for it. He had many opportunities to knock down the opposition, yet he lost the election. Many will say that he lost because of Perot, but if he had been stronger, Perot might not have been around at all. Many Republicans felt that he did not work hard enough to get reelected.

MR. BOLTON: My own view is that Bush lost because of his 1990 "read my lips" promise not to raise taxes. People believed him and took him at his word. When he failed to keep it, he had a problem.

I certainly know the image of the frenetic public speaker who cannot finish his sentences, but I never saw President Bush like that in private. I always saw him as detached and low key. Bush had a technocratic view of government, as illustrated by the members of his domestic Cabinet. Nevertheless, they all had the same kind of approach to things that he did, which I think cost him domestically. It cost him the core of the Republican party, which would have liked to have seen a more fired-up president and candidate.

NARRATOR: Did you ever see evidence of a health problem?

MR. BOLTON: No, not at all.

QUESTION: Were there discussions or decisions about what the administration policy would be if he failed to get authorization for the use of force at the United Nations or on Capitol Hill?

MR. BOLTON: I was told to figure out how to get the authorization, and if I could not do so, to return and tell them soon.

Another illustration of diplomacy without ambassadors is how the United States works the Security Council members in Washington, their capitals, and New York, all at the same time. I met with the Finnish ambassador about once or twice a week before the invasion of Kuwait and every week following that invasion. By mid-October, our final conclusion was that Security Council authorization was probable but not certain. At that point, Baker talked to the President and decided that he would pay a personal visit to every foreign minister whose country was on the Security Council. Baker planned to tell them the language that the United States proposed to use and ask them if they would support it. Baker wanted a face-to-face commitment from them to vote with the United States. That way, the administration could go down the list of countries on the Security Council and be fairly certain how they would vote.

I remember getting to the bottom of the list, and Baker—who is nothing if not a good vote counter—saying that there had better be the needed nine votes. He said that he did not want to go to the Security Council only to be missing a vote or to have China veto it. When he said that, there wasn't a doubt in my mind that he would fire me immediately if the votes did not come through. The administration could not afford to lose that vote, which is why—forgetting ambassadors and staff—Baker made it his personal responsibility to see the foreign minister of each and every member of the Security Council, including the foreign minister of Cuba in New York. The day before the vote, Baker took Cuba's foreign minister to the Waldorf and gave a very effective pitch in favor of the resolution.

Though it did not have any effect on the Cubans, Baker's efforts illustrate how far it is necessary to go just to avoid exactly the predicament you described in your question—that is, to avoid not getting the authorization to use force.

Some people might say it was a question of trying to get the Security Council authorization and that if the United States did not do so, it would just do what it wanted anyway. As for myself, though I agree that the administration probably would have proceeded as planned even without the authorization, it was never an either/or question. The bottom line was that the administration had to get the vote.

In terms of congressional politics, one reason they waited until January was to make sure the votes existed. It was a political exercise with the same conclusion; that is, the administration did not want to have a situation in which it lacked congressional authorization.

QUESTION: Several years ago, shortly after the Argentina-U.K. confrontation, a retiring admiral of the NATO fleet said that Britain's response to the Falklands was the most perfect example of how international conflict should be handled: The issue arose, and it was debated in the Parliament. The political objective was decided, and Prime Minister Thatcher energized the so-called public will. No discussion about it was held at home because the political will had been determined ahead of time by the legislative process. The retiring admiral said that he was sorry the American process could not be as simple. (Of course, Thatcher had also delegated the affair to one admiral, only to have a ship carrying 250 sailors sink, thus creating a terrible incident.) Would you comment on the differences between the decision-making processes of Great Britain and the United States on matters like Desert Storm?

MR. BOLTON: Your example illustrates the fundamental difference between a parliamentary system and a system of separated powers. In the first system, assuming a majority in the Parliament, that kind of political decision could be made and separated from implementation. As I said, the Bush administration benefited from the fact of Congress's lack of a major role in his Desert Storm decision. That is the U.S. system for better or worse, and situations will arise in which an administration will not have that luxury.

For example, on Central American policy, one of the things Bush and Baker decided at the very beginning was that they did not want to fight with Congress on Central America. Remember that Iran-contra had debilitated much of the Reagan administration's foreign policy ability. The State Department and Congress are barely on speaking terms when it comes to Central America. Central America was a case where the opinion of Congress was very centrally involved right from the beginning. For that reason Baker went to Capitol Hill early on to discuss what kind of resolution could be worked out on a negotiated basis. The end of the Cold War made it easier to get this happy ending. Central America is the perfect example of an area in which congressional views were very much involved. By virtue of the U.S. system of separated powers, every administration has to live with and adjust to Congress's role in making foreign policy. Nevertheless, there is a difference between taking Congress's views into account and seeing Congress as an equal partner in decision making.

When I was at the Justice Department during Iran-contra, the House Foreign Affairs Committee called CIA Director William Casey to testify. About three of us were in the audience. I was there to listen to what Casey had to say not from a prosecutorial point of view at the Justice Department, but because the Justice Department was curious about what the CIA had been doing. Dante Fascell, the chairman of the Foreign Affairs Committee at the time, introduced Casey, and he talked about how the committee had questions about what President Reagan was thinking, what the President heard from his senior advisers in the administration, and what the President had heard from his senior advisers in Congress. That was the embodiment of the misconception. The President does not have any senior advisers in Congress. He has senior advisers in his administration, but Congress is a separate branch of government, not the President's second Cabinet. It is an important distinction to recognize.

NARRATOR: Thank you, Mr. Bolton, for your clear and instructive presentation, not only on the Bush presidency but on the whole approach to foreign policy decision making in the United States.

CHAPTER 7

THE BUSH PRESIDENCY AND INTERNATIONAL ECONOMIC ISSUES*

DAVID C. MULFORD

NARRATOR: Dr. David Mulford is vice chairman and a member of the executive board of CS First Boston, Inc., and chairman of CS First Boston Europe. From 1984 to 1992 he served as under-secretary and assistant secretary of international affairs in the Department of the Treasury. He was the senior international economic policy official in that department during the terms of secretaries Regan, Baker, and Brady. During that time Dr. Mulford led the development of the United States' international debt strategy and President Bush's Enterprise Initiative (EI) for the Americas. Among other responsibilities and accomplishments, he headed the U.S. delegation to negotiate the establishment of the European Bank for Reconstruction and Development and the G-7 negotiations to reduce Poland's bilateral debt.

Dr. Mulford holds several degrees. He received a doctorate from Oxford University, a master's degree in political science from Boston University, and a bachelor's degree in economics from Lawrence University. He received an honorary Doctor of Laws degree from Lawrence University in 1984, the Legion d'Honneur from French President Francois Mitterrand in 1990, the Distinguished Alumni Award from Boston University in 1992, and the Order of May for Merit from Argentine President Carlos Saul

---

*Presented in a Forum at the Miller Center of Public Affairs on 4 October 1995.

Menem in 1993. He is now a member of the Council on Foreign Relations and works with the Center for Strategic and International Studies in Washington.

MR. MULFORD: I would like to begin by explaining my background because it is often useful to understand the speaker's perspective. After earning my Ph.D. at Oxford, I was a White House fellow from 1965 to 1966, the first year of the White House fellowship program. That experience proved to be very formative for me because I spent my year at the Treasury Department with Treasury Secretary Henry Fowler and Undersecretary of the Treasury Joe Barr. Then I went into the international financial business, working at White, Weld & Co., for 18 years. For nine of those years, I was the financial adviser to the Saudi government. This was the time during which they were eagerly searching for places to invest their enormous oil revenues.

I acquired an unusual view of the world economy and world financial markets as they were developing during that formative period. In 1984, I was asked by Don Regan, then-secretary of the treasury, to take the international job in the Treasury Department because he felt that I knew a great deal about international money flows, which were becoming more and more important. I was delighted to have that opportunity. I went to Washington in the last year of the first Reagan administration and continued to serve in the Treasury Department during the second Reagan administration and then during the Bush administration, a total of nine years. When I left, I was told that this tenure made me the longest serving presidential appointee at the Treasury Department in this century.

At the end of the Bush administration, I returned to the business of international finance. I now spend my time working on a global basis, which involves a great deal of travel, and am involved in the highly visible kinds of transactions where public policy and finance interface—namely, in large-scale privatization programs. I am therefore a person from the private sector who has spent some time in government and has a strong public policy interest, but I am not a lifetime government person.

I would next like to make a few general points about George Bush. First, I have clear views of George Bush from my memories of working with him. In my opinion, he is, above all, an outstanding American person in every way. He was, as some people have put it, a very decent person. My experience with him was that he was a kind and considerate person despite being under the pressure of serving as head of state. I believe he had the right values to be the national leader of the United States.

George Bush was renowned for his strong interest and talents in foreign policy. From my perspective on the economic side of those issues, he was enormously knowledgeable and always conducted himself as a professional. He was particularly strong in the policy formation process. He understood how the U.S. government works and how other governments work. George Bush also had a sense of history and understood where the United States fit into the history of the Western world. He had a great deal of experience in the field, liked foreign policy, and knew how policies were generated within a government. This unique strength stood in direct contrast to Ronald Reagan, who did not have either those interests or the inclination to spend his time in the policy-making process, even though he was a formidable president and head of state. George Bush obviously had some weaknesses, but I think he made a major contribution and will be seen by history as an important president.

The achievements on international economic issues are on the short list of the Bush administration's policy initiatives that will be noted as lasting accomplishments in years to come. Oddly enough, it is not an area that receives much attention. That oversight is due to the lack of interest on the part of the U.S. news media and elected public officials, many of whom are more interested in foreign policy issues. Nevertheless, looking ahead 10 or 15 years, the accomplishments in the international economic area during the Bush administration will have a greater impact on this country. I am referring particularly to the initiatives that President Bush made in the area of international debt, especially in Latin America.

An extremely serious problem of indebtedness on the part of the countries of Latin America suddenly came into the foreground in 1982. Mexico in effect defaulted on its debt in August 1982, followed by payment lapses on the part of Brazil and virtually every other country in Latin America except Colombia. This event deeply shook the international financial system because banks in the United States and elsewhere had lent heavily to these countries (U.S. banks accounted for about 32 percent of the total amount of these loans). It was truly an international problem that threatened the stability of the international financial system and the U.S. banking system in a very real way. For a while things were extremely delicate. I was not yet in government at that time, but if those events had not been appropriately addressed, they might have caused an international financial crisis. A scenario reminiscent of the Great Depression could then have resulted in this country.

The first approach of the U.S. government in the wake of the debt crisis was simply to muddle through and try to keep the system together by encouraging banks not to cut lines of credit or withdraw their loans and to continue to make credit available to these countries even though they could not meet their obligations. In the fall of 1985 Secretary of the Treasury Jim Baker undertook an initiative called the Baker Plan, which I helped to develop. The Baker Plan aimed in a more formal way at trying to keep the banks engaged in these debtor countries. It sought to make new money available under "forced" lending operations, under which the great syndicates (which sometimes included 400 to 500 banks) would be persuaded to provide new credit to the countries and roll over their existing debts to keep them afloat. At the same time, the countries were all being encouraged to initiate programs with the International Monetary Fund (IMF) to reform their economies and restore the basis for growth so they could eventually manage this debt. This strategy wasn't working, however. Basically, the accumulated stock of debt was just being rolled over or rescheduled into the future and thus continued to grow relentlessly.

Latin American countries were falling into a deeper recession after 1982, with both high unemployment and high inflation. The United States government became very worried about the political stability of these countries. The conventional wisdom at the time was that if the economic strains got too bad, they would succumb either to a Communist takeover or a right-wing dictatorship. History in Latin America would repeat itself and would have a detrimental effect on the U.S. economy because the United States had built up a major trading relationship with these countries. Unlike U.S. trade with other parts of the world, which was heavily damaged during the period when the dollar was strong, the United States continued to enjoy strong trade relations with Latin America in manufactured goods, the bread and butter of American industry, and U.S. exports accounted for a major share of those markets. When those countries went into recession, they therefore had a negative impact on these traditional industries in the United States, exacerbating the ongoing loss of jobs.

The 1980s are now referred to as the "lost decade" in Latin America because the economic problems were completely overwhelming for these countries. There seemed to be no way out of this situation because even if they did recover and begin to grow again, they were so overburdened by this vast pile of debt that they would never be able to escape it and put their economies on a solid base again.

When George Bush was elected in November 1988, one of the first issues that he addressed with then-Treasury Secretary Nicholas Brady was this so-called Latin American debt problem. (In fact, it also affected Poland, Central Europe, and various other countries.) We then began work on what later became the Brady Plan. It was a very concentrated exercise. President-elect Bush called together a group composed of Secretary of State Jim Baker, National Security Adviser Brent Scowcroft, Federal Reserve Chairman Alan Greenspan, Office of Management and Budget Director Dick Darman, and Nick Brady. I was the "ideas" person and secretary of the group.

We faced a complicated problem because to solve it, the debt had to be reduced—that is, forgiven. That decision would set a bad precedent for the U.S. domestic economy, however. The United States has a high degree of indebtedness both as a nation and from individuals. If the U.S. government forgives the debt of a foreign country, how does it explain that action to its own citizens who are indebted to the government? On the other hand, unless the debt problem was addressed promptly, private banks would withdraw from the market. They were starting to sell their loans to investors in the market or other banks, and some European banks were deciding to absorb the losses and write them off. An extreme lack of consensus existed within the world banking community. If that situation continued, more and more of the debt would have to be assumed by intergovernmental organizations like the World Bank and the IMF. This indebtedness would gradually accumulate in the hands of governments and ultimately become the responsibility of taxpayers like ourselves. That long-term prognosis was clearly unacceptable and also threatened the system. These inherent dilemmas were extremely difficult to resolve.

By December 1988 George Bush had decided he would launch the proposal of this group—the so-called Brady Plan, in which resources of the IMF and the World Bank and those of various governments were to be used to provide collateral backing for debt. For example, U.S. Treasury bonds with a 30-year maturity would be bought by debtor governments with official resources and pledged as security collateral for the bank debt at sharply reduced values. Holders of the debt would in turn be forced to write the debt down to the discounted level or to receive lower levels of interest to reduce their debt burden on an equivalent basis. For example, if a bank had $100 worth of debt with Mexico, it might be offered $70 worth of new secured debts in exchange. It would therefore take a write-off of $30, but the new $70 of debt it received would be backed by U.S. Treasury securities, making it more secure. The Mexicans would buy those U.S. Treasury zero coupon bonds at a deep discount and use them as collateral for the remaining loans. After 30 years when the bonds matured at their full principal value and were paid off by the U.S. government, the Mexican government would use the proceeds to pay off its own rescheduled debt. The U.S. taxpayer would incur no costs at all because if the Treasury zero coupon bonds were not bought by Mexico, they would be bought by other investors, such as individual Americans, pension funds, or by other institutional investors.

The point is that Mr. Bush had to stand up to the banks and explain that in order to enjoy this benefit of greater security, they would have to take a substantial one-time write-down, which was very painful for them. That aspect was very controversial when the plan was announced by Mr. Brady in March 1989. Other complex provisions were included in the plan to use resources to help in the reduction of debt. The President had to decide that he would support the debt reduction plan even though homeowners, farmers, veterans, students, and various other groups owed approximately $150 to $160 billion to the U.S. government, and their loan debts would not be forgiven. This aspect of the Brady Plan was controversial, but Bush realized the desperate importance of restoring Latin America before it became a permanently depressed region in this hemisphere, thus damaging U.S. national security and long-term economic prospects.

Four months after the plan was announced, Mexico negotiated the first deal. Its foreign debt was reduced by 17 percent, and a most extraordinary transformation occurred. Once debtor countries demonstrated that the pattern of constant debt accumulation was not going to continue but instead would level off and decline, they regained investor confidence. Within a short period of time, private money began to flow back into Mexico, and economic vitality was restored. The same pattern emerged in the next couple of years throughout Latin America, which once again became the fastest area of export growth for the United States. This meant an increase in jobs in the U.S. economy, which was then in an extended period of recession or low growth. In other words, these developments had a clear and positive impact on Main Street America.

The effect since then has been even more surprising. Instead of returning to its cycle of revolution, collapse, and recovery, Latin America has enjoyed an extended period of growth, stability, democratization, investment, and rising trade. Much of this transformation can be attributed to the successful resolution of the debt problem. George Bush then followed the Brady Plan with the Enterprise Initiative for the Americas, which aimed at stimulating investment and trade while still addressing the official government debt problems of the smaller countries of Latin America. It was announced in 1991 and proved to have a dramatic impact on this hemisphere. Whereas in the past, most of the relations were North-South between the United States and various countries, the EI committed the United States over a period of years to increased freedom of trade and investment within the region and ultimately the creation of a free-trade area in the entire hemisphere. The initiative also included incentives for those countries to open their investment regimes and allow private capital to move more freely.

The effect of Bush's strategy was the most dramatic in Mexico. The North American Free Trade Agreement (NAFTA) was negotiated during the Bush administration and promulgated during President Clinton's first year in office. Mexico has passed Japan and become the United States' second largest trading partner after Canada—a very significant change. Costa Rica, Honduras, and other Caribbean countries also made economic recoveries as their stock of official debt was reduced. George Bush understood the importance of the common traditions of democracy, religion, and culture in this hemisphere in addition to the economic interrelationships. He thus knew he had to deal with the debt problem effectively in a very short period of time.

New trade relations have developed between Latin American countries that did not trade extensively with each other before, and they continue to grow in size and importance. The idea of George Bush that this hemisphere should have a common trading system will one day become a reality. Central American and Caribbean countries will look for ways to associate with the NAFTA arrangements in Mexico. In due course, I have no doubt that the transformation of this hemisphere toward greater economic integration will continue. This development will not entail giving up sovereignty or adopting a single currency as the European Union is trying to do, but it will bring increasingly common policies on trade and investment. This period of history is generally one of growing insecurity in the world inasmuch as the fading away of the superpower rivalries of the Cold War gives rise to more frequent local conflicts. In Latin America, these changes will provide the United States with an area of stability and rapid growth in the Western hemisphere in many ways rivaling Southeast Asia. It may not be quite as strong as Southeast Asia, but it will be an important long-term benefit to the United States.

Just as he did in Latin America, George Bush also recognized the importance of addressing the indebtedness of Poland. When the Berlin Wall fell and the Soviet Empire was collapsing, Poland was heavily indebted, much more than the Czech Republic, Hungary, and the other countries of Eastern Europe. Unlike Latin American countries, however, most of that was not bank debt; it was money owed to governments that had provided loans in the 1980s. Poland had not been able to honor those debts. Once again, George Bush stood up in the Group of Seven (G-7) and insisted that the Polish debt problem be addressed by the governments. That plan to forgive a portion of Polish debt took a long time to negotiate, but in the end a 50 percent debt reduction was granted to Poland in 1991. Since then, Poland's economy has been growing at a positive rate up to 9 percent per year. President Bush's leadership saved the day, lifting the Polish people's hopes at a critical time.

Owing seemingly insurmountable debt can be a demoralizing experience, a feeling that one can never escape. The effect on countries' psyches is just as profound as it is for families or individuals. This sense of hopelessness undermines national institutions while high unemployment and high inflation demoralizes populations even further. Addressing these debt problems was therefore a very important foreign policy issue.

Another example of George Bush's foresight was seen in his attitude toward the Soviet Union and Russia. Although the Soviet Union had a large, technologically sophisticated economy, when it broke up it was heavily indebted to Western banks and governments, especially Italy, France, and Germany. Only a modest debt was owed to the U.S. government. In the first winter after the failed coup attempt in August 1991, there was a great deal of concern about insufficient medical supplies and food supplies in Russia. Press coverage centered on potential revolution and the prospects of Russian people starving in the streets. In the final days of the Soviet Union, I was sent to Moscow with my counterparts in other major countries to discuss debt servicing with Mr. Gorbachev and his successors in the government of Russia. Under the legislation governing difficult credits in most countries, no new credit can be extended to a country if it is not servicing its existing debt. U.S. legislation requires that credit be cut off if a country fails to pay on an outstanding debt it already owes to the U.S. government. Russia became insolvent during that period; it did not have enough money to meet its interest payments to foreign governments.

George Bush understood that it was important to solve that issue very early and also to encourage other countries to immediately admit Russia and the other former Soviet republics into the World Bank and the IMF. Again, that suggestion was not initially supported by heads of state in Europe who thought the Russians should wait longer, but George Bush insisted, and like Poland, these countries were admitted. In Mr. Bush's view, by becoming full members instead of associates or mere recipients, these countries would feel they had a stake in these institutions and could begin to learn how the world's market economy works. They would get some of the benefits of belonging to these institutions and begin to exercise some of the necessary discipline.

Whether Russia likes it or not, the Russian economy is integrating with the global economy for the first time (It had been isolated as a planned economy). Thus, domestic economic policy issues, whether in the United States or Russia, can no longer be handled in isolation or without regard to what is happening in the global economy. Russia is very much caught up in this process of integration at the moment and is going through a painful but so far reasonably positive adjustment.

Once again, George Bush had the foresight to help facilitate Russian economic adjustments even before the Berlin Wall fell. In 1989 he asked three or four of us in the administration to meet regularly with a group of Russian senior economic policy people whom he invited to Washington. We spent two or three days with them in the Executive Office Building listening to their reform plans and trying to educate them about the Western economy. It was a strange experience because the first people who came were functionaries or bureaucrats out of the Soviet system who had learned the terminology of Western economics but did not understand what the words meant. For example, they would occasionally ask me who really set the prices in the United States. That is a hard question to answer because the market sets prices. They did not believe that there was not someone in Washington setting prices as they did in Moscow. Those people changed as the Soviet system collapsed, but that relationship was crucial during the transition period from 1989 to 1991. In my opinion that effort will go down again as another lasting accomplishment of George Bush.

This discussion has hopefully provided a sense of the day-to-day, key issues we faced in the Bush administration. Through these experiences, I learned the high priority that George Bush gave to addressing these issues because he did get personally involved at the key moments. He had the expertise to understand fully the details of what was being done, often made major contributions to developing policy, and was able to effectively oversee the implementation of that policy.

NARRATOR: How did George Bush prepare himself to handle complex economic policy issues such as the Latin American debt problem?

MR. MULFORD: George Bush would have categorized the Latin American debt problem as a foreign policy problem with an economic dimension to it. During his travels as vice president, Latin American heads of state had begged him to address the debt problem before it destroyed the hemisphere. The fact is that when staff discussions got into detailed aspects of economic policy, he was not very interested. Looking back on his administration, this lack of deep involvement in economic issues is one of the reasons why his domestic policy was not as successful. He was very knowledgeable about foreign policy and grasped the importance of international economic issues. When the small meetings of the Brady Plan group in the White House were held, he would become personally involved because those issues affected foreign policy, unlike purely domestic economic issues. He was more engaged when foreign policy and economics went together, and he understood the implications of solving the debt problem for the U.S. position in this hemisphere.

QUESTION: Based on the Latin American experience, is it reasonable to hope that private capital will flow to Eastern Europe without substantial government guarantees?

MR. MULFORD: Yes, and indeed capital already *is* flowing to Russia and Central Europe. George Bush understood that to put a country back on its feet, the economic reform process has to begin at home. It has to have a domestic political basis, and it has to be supported by the people. That support often becomes available when people are frightened of inflation or being unemployed; they do not like getting poorer. The politician must address those concerns to get a consensus.

Reforms began to take effect in many Latin American countries before the Brady Plan and have greatly accelerated since. They privatized government-run companies, dismantled tariff barriers, welcomed outside investment, and reduced tax rates. Those reforms in Latin America, particularly in Mexico, began around 1985 and formed the basis that allowed the development of a solid debt strategy. Those countries were already becoming attractive to foreign capital, but the debt burden had to be lightened to attract further investment. When the debt was reduced, capital rushed in. George Bush understood the connection between these areas and the prospects for recovery in Latin America. The same potential for economic development is there in Central Europe and Russia. I am optimistic about the long-run investment prospects because Russians are hard workers and highly trained.

During my service in the government, I found that many officials still held to the old notion that the United States was the dominant player in the world because of its military superiority. I believe, however, that economic competition has become the decisive factor in the post-Cold War era.

QUESTION: Mr. Bush was criticized during the 1992 campaign for not devoting as much attention to the problems of the inner cities in the United States as he did to the problems of Latin America. Are some of the principles that were developed in the Brady Plan applicable to the inner cities?

MR. MULFORD: The point you are making is valid, and I would broaden it to encompass more than just the inner cities. During the Cold War the United States had spent 40 years investing in global security and leading a long-term foreign policy program that was aimed at defeating Communist dictatorship. The collapse of the Berlin Wall, the breakup of the Soviet Union, and the victory in the Gulf War basically mark that victory, but a tremendous cost was borne by this country in terms of the reallocation of resources. In retrospect, it does seem strange that more attention was not paid following the above events to the challenge of immediately restoring the United States. Over a year passed between the Gulf War and the 1992 campaign, by which time strengthening the domestic economy had become a central issue. An opportunity was lost to turn the focus back to the United States and challenge the American people to restore this country. The inner cities are part of that challenge.

Many of the techniques used in Latin America could indeed be used to help in the inner cities, but the most effective reforms in Latin America are broad policies that cover the whole country. For example, Chile and Argentina have established private pension systems, whereas the United States has not reformed its Social Security system. Likewise, Latin American labor laws are being made less restrictive to provide better job opportunities. These are the kinds of broad policy reforms that help provide freedom to areas that are having trouble, such as America's inner cities. Such domestic problems are very different politically, so neither President Bush nor his advisers looked at them in the same way that they did in assisting reform programs abroad. You are nevertheless making an important point that as the world integrates, the solutions for many of these problems will increasingly tend to be transferable.

NARRATOR: Mr. Mulford, just back from Mexico, has made an extraordinary sacrifice in coming to speak today. He has been one of the most gracious people with whom we have dealt, and his colleagues speak very highly of him. We are grateful to him for today's presentation.

V

THE INTELLIGENCE
PROCESS

CHAPTER 8

INTELLIGENCE IN THE REAGAN AND BUSH PRESIDENCIES*

ROBERT M. GATES

NARRATOR: Robert Gates was director of central intelligence from 1991 to 1993. He came to that position with a breadth of experience. Dr. Gates has held various positions in the Central Intelligence Agency (CIA) since 1966, including deputy director for intelligence, chairman of the National Intelligence Council, and deputy director of central intelligence. He earned a doctorate in Russian and Soviet history at Georgetown University and held positions on the National Security Council staff under three presidents. In January 1989 President Bush named Dr. Gates assistant to the president and deputy for national security affairs, working with a friend of the Miller Center, General Brent Scowcroft. Following that, in 1991 he was confirmed and appointed director of central intelligence.

Since leaving the government he has been a director of several Fortune 500 corporations and has been a senior adviser to other boards. He is a member of the board of trustees of the Forum for International Policy. We count it a great privilege that he would be with us this morning and an equally great privilege that former Secretary of State Lawrence Eagleburger has joined us for this discussion.

Presented in a Forum at the Miller Center of Public Affairs on 18 October 1993.

MR. GATES: I think the kind of history that the Miller Center is putting together is very important. I have had the opportunity to serve four presidents in the White House and to work under six at CIA.

As I reflect on this experience, there are a couple of themes I think are germane. First, our political process disguises from our citizens the essential continuity in policy between our presidents, and the news media do not contribute in this respect. Throughout the history of the administrations of Nixon, Ford, Carter, and Reagan, politicians felt their interests were served by highlighting presidential differences. In reality, however, there was a great deal of continuity. This was especially true in foreign policy and in terms of dealing with the Soviet Union. In that respect, I believe that the Vietnam syndrome was overstated, and with the exception of some quarters of the Department of Defense and Capitol Hill, no U.S. president, including President Carter, was inhibited from the use of force when they felt it served the national interest and demonstrated our engagement in the Third World.

It is also important to understand how important the presidency is in our government and the degree to which the pressures and responsibilities felt by the president are unique to our system. I developed a great deal of respect for all six presidents for whom I worked. One must work closely enough with presidents to see how much they give of themselves to the job and how much they care, and this is true regardless of which president we choose as an example. They tend to be uniformly treated badly while in office by the public and by the press. The criticism has nothing to do with their politics. It is because they are there and because they are the president.

NARRATOR: Some years ago in an article you wrote for the *Washington Quarterly*, you pointed out that little has been written on the impact of intelligence on presidential decision making. In view of your service under General Scowcroft, could you shed light on this issue? How important is intelligence to foreign policy decision making? Your insights are significant because some, like Senator Moynihan from New York, are arguing that CIA is obsolete and its functions could be assumed by the State Department. Is that practical in your view?

MR. GATES: There is a tremendous misunderstanding in the public arena about the role of intelligence. One of the reasons I took a number of initiatives to begin opening up intelligence archives in 1992 was to give scholars the access they need to evaluate the role of intelligence in history properly. Recently, more than 250 National Intelligence Estimates (NIEs) relating to Europe, Berlin, Germany, Russia, and the Soviet Union were declassified and made available to the public as the first major step in the program. Most of the NIEs from the late 1940s and the 1950s have already been declassified. All of the estimates on the Soviet Union through 1983 will be reviewed for declassification.

The public dialogue about the role of intelligence has focused primarily on two areas: covert action and large estimates of the future. I think, however, that neither of those areas constitute what has been the enduring strength of the American intelligence system.

Covert action has played a role. I notice in many histories that American support for the restoration of Iran's shah in 1953 is regarded as a transitory solution. I think the United States and the other industrialized countries would be gratified if they could find today a "transitory" solution to Persian Gulf instability that would last for a quarter of a century. Covert action also played a significant role in keeping hope alive in the Soviet Union and Eastern Europe. I think that France and Germany are free today because of covert actions after World War II that gave democratic parties the resources to deal with Communist parties. We also played an important role in Afghanistan and other places. There is no question, however, that some real disasters have occurred.

In trying to forecast the future beyond five years, one would probably do about as well with the psychic Jeane Dixon as with a NIE. We have had some terrific successes, however, such as our forecasts on the 1967 Middle East war and on qualitative improvements in Soviet weapons systems. We have also had some real disasters, including the November 1989 NIE, which concluded that Saddam Hussein would focus on rebuilding his domestic infrastructure for the next three years. NIEs, however, are not considered to be the most important factor in policy-making. In my experience, NIEs are more or less disregarded by senior policymakers. A NIE either reaffirms what the policymaker already believed, or if the policymaker does not agree with it, he doesn't let it influence his judgment.

The sustaining force for bipartisan support on Capitol Hill for a robust U.S. intelligence capability comes from what I call the daily "river of information" that flows to the policy community. It is this daily information that tells policymakers the status of the 30,000-plus nuclear weapons in Russia; how long the runways are in Somalia; where the death camps are in Bosnia; the progress of the North Koreans on their nuclear weapons program; the Iranian rearmament program and the sophisticated weapons the Iranians are buying from the Russians, including three Kilo-class submarines. The river of information has guided inspectors looking for weapons of mass destruction in Iraq; has tracked the South African nuclear program; has dealt with conventional weapons production all over the world; and has monitored the collusion of foreign governments and foreign companies, which tends to disadvantage U.S. business.

This regular flow of millions of pieces of information that is integrated and presented to policymakers every day is in my opinion the prime value of our intelligence community. I think it has played a critical role in our ability to make informed decisions, particularly in guiding crisis management and overall policy directions. This flow of information is far more critical than any of the specific estimates that were done.

Information was made available to the Nixon administration, for example, showing that the Soviets were building a submarine base in Cuba in 1970. Many similar instances could be cited that would demonstrate the primary contribution of our intelligence community. The value of intelligence is continuing. We now see American intelligence being used to support U.N. peacekeepers in Somalia, Bosnia, Cambodia, and elsewhere, as well as to support the International Atomic Energy Agency (IAEA) in its nuclear inspections around the world. An example symbolizing this change in the audience for American intelligence was captured in a briefing done for the U.N. Security Council by a U.S. intelligence officer. This officer was briefing the Russians, Chinese, and others sitting at the table using a satellite photograph marked "no foreign dissemination." Thus, we have a little cultural catching up to do in that respect. Nevertheless, it is this river of information and the ability to manage it independent of any policy preference axes to grind that makes the continuing contribution of intelligence quite clear. This view is supported by both the Clinton administration—which put forward to Capitol Hill a very satisfactory intelligence budget—and Congress.

We need to keep a historical perspective. There is a great deal of talk now suggesting that many agencies of government around Washington are relics of the Cold War. It is true that many institutions were created in 1947, including the Air Force, the Joint Chiefs of Staff, and the CIA. But while their creation may have been sparked by the Cold War, early on they became instruments of American international leadership everywhere—not just focused on the Soviet Union. At the high point of the Cold War in terms of CIA spending on the Soviet target—incidentally, that was in 1980, in terms of percentage—more than two-fifths of the U.S. intelligence budget was spent on issues and problems that had nothing to do with the Soviet Union. In the last budget I submitted for fiscal year 1993, CIA's total expenditure on the Soviet or the Russian target (including the others within the Confederation of Independent States) was only 13 percent, one-third for the overall intelligence community. A large proportion of our intelligence effort has always been devoted to non-Soviet problems, and that obviously continues to this day.

NARRATOR: Was your work affected by the fact that President Bush had been director of central intelligence?

MR. GATES: It is always discomforting to know that your boss has done your job. In fact, we used to kid around and tell our young Agency trainees that since Yuri Andropov became general-secretary of the Soviet Communist party and Bush became vice president and then president, it showed that a good intelligence officer could rise to any position.

President Bush probably had a better appreciation than any of his predecessors for what intelligence could and could not do. I think many of his predecessors had exaggerated expectations about what could be done with covert action, for example, and how the CIA could predict the future even when those leaders whose actions were being predicted had not made up their minds as to what course to take. At the same time, President Bush's predecessors often underestimated what U.S. intelligence could do, revealing an ambivalence that arose from a lack of understanding. President

Bush from the first day had a thorough understanding of the capabilities of U.S. intelligence and where it could be improved.

I would say that one of the nice things is that President Bush never interfered in the slightest way in the day-to-day management of intelligence. Like all of his predecessors since the creation of U.S. intelligence, he complained when he was surprised by some event overseas. By and large, I think his understanding of what we could do was his greatest asset. Otherwise, he pretty much stayed out of the management of the business.

QUESTION: I am curious about this "river of information." There also are rivers of information coming out of the Department of State and the Pentagon. What distinguishes these rivers? Is there a duplication of effort?

MR. GATES: The river of information in each of the other departments tends to flow in the first instance to support that department's own secretary and the activities of that organization.

The CIA was created in 1947 for two purposes, and I think those two purposes continue to remain valid. The first one drew on the lesson of Pearl Harbor, where information that could have warned of the attack was available but was not brought together in an effective way and was not presented to anyone who could make decisions. One of the purposes of the creation of CIA was to have an organization whose job it was to gather information from every element of the government and from its own resources and to integrate that information and provide it directly to the president, to whom it was solely responsible. The structure alleviated the worry that there might have been information out there in the hands of a governmental agency or branch of the armed forces that had not been brought to the attention of senior policymakers outside of the originating department. It also provided a place where in-house information could be combined with information from other departments and presented to the National Security Council and the president. This integrative function of all of these rivers is one of the two primary purposes of CIA and the U.S. intelligence community.

The second purpose for founding CIA was to create an organization—although possibly having its own biases—that was not biased in favor of a particular policy or was not trying to protect its own departmental policy activities. CIA has made some mistakes over time. The Congress did not want the Defense Department to be the only source of information about the Soviet threat, convinced that if this were the case, the threat would be exaggerated to justify its own budget. We reached a point in the mid-to-late 1980s where Senator Nunn and others on the Hill often would turn to CIA when the Department of Defense brought a new weapons system to the Congress for approval, and say, "We want you to evaluate this proposed weapon system before we approve it. We want you to evaluate the Soviet threat against which this weapon is being designed."

In another case, the Congress became suspicious of the Navy's claims that the Soviets had made no progress in their antisubmarine warfare programs. The Congress was worried that the Soviets might in fact have created some new technologies and capabilities that the Navy simply was not willing to recognize and take seriously. The Congress gave CIA literally tens of millions of dollars over a period of years to do an independent analysis of the Soviet antisubmarine warfare capability to give them confidence that they had an honest and unbiased account of the threat. On the other hand, the Congress did not want the Department of State evaluating the effectiveness of its policies in one or another country.

CIA over time has had its own biases. For example, CIA seriously underestimated the number of Intercontinental Ballistic Missiles (ICBMs) that the Soviets were deploying during the 1960s. In the 1970s, and perhaps in the early 1980s, there were overestimates in some cases. Often there were both over and underestimates, but it was usually based on the available information rather than a particular policy bias.

CIA's two major functions were therefore to integrate information from the government and all over the world and to ensure that the president and Congress were getting accurate information on world events. I think those are still valid reasons for CIA's existence. The truth of the matter is that all of the departments of government in the national security arena participate in the intelligence community and both give and receive information.

Everyone has heard about CIA's role in covert action over the years, but people do not realize how very critical the intelligence community was to the arms control process. U.S.-Soviet negotiations over a period of 25 years took place on the basis of information provided by U.S. intelligence because the Soviets would not provide any information. You probably have heard the story, which is not apocryphal, that one of the Soviet military officials on their arms control delegation once told our delegation to stop talking about Soviet weapons in front of Soviet civilians because they weren't cleared to know such information. Our support for the negotiations managed by the State Department and our ability to monitor agreements once reached made the entire process possible and made possible ratification of those arms control agreements. Thus, while the director of central intelligence's primary customer is the president, he in fact serves the entire policy community.

NARRATOR: Secretary Eagleburger, do you have a comment about the Bush presidency?

MR. EAGLEBURGER: He did a pretty good job. I have never believed the State Department should be doing the CIA's job—not on the question of analysis and certainly not on the question of covert activities. I think Senator Moynihan is just wrong if he thinks the State Department could or should do it. The CIA is not always unbiased, as Dr. Gates said, but—particularly if the State Department has a policy in mind—I would not want my analysis of the intelligence to be done by someone who was trying to beef up the policy. I think caution in this area is terribly important.

It is also reversible. When the CIA was created, Dean Acheson insisted on the creation of an intelligence research function within the State Department as a counterweight to what the CIA might produce so that the secretary of state could have his own independent analysis. I think that is a good idea, and I think Dr. Gates, to some degree, would agree. All of the agencies put their materials into the intelligence process and arrive at a National Intelligence Estimate, which on occasion tends to be the least common denominator. At times there are substantial differences of view, and it is important that those differences be aired. One of those issues where I suspect there is still a substantial degree of difference between the CIA and the State Department is on what the North Koreans are up to with regard to the nuclear issue. I always thought—despite the fact that I was in the State Department—that the State Department grossly underestimated the danger, and that in fact, the CIA was much closer to the mark. In the course of the last few months I think we have learned that the Agency was much closer to the truth than the State Department. You need some competition, some battling back and forth with ideas. I would hate to see everything subsumed into the State Department. We would run intelligence about as well as we do foreign aid!

MR. GATES: My experience with Senator Moynihan over the years has been that sometimes he will exaggerate to make a point. As vice chairman of the Senate Select Committee on Intelligence, Senator Moynihan played a constructive and helpful role in the rebuilding of the intelligence community after the late 1970s. I am not sure how serious Senator Moynihan is in saying that the intelligence apparatus can be dismantled. If he means to say that it needs to change and it needs to be restructured to deal with a new world, I think he is right.

QUESTION: Given the rumors circulating lately that Israel was shipping our arms technology to China, how long do you think we can afford to pay the price for that?

MR. GATES: One of the areas that is awkward to talk about publicly is our intelligence relationships with other countries. I have always believed that it is a mistake to depend too much on any one individual source for information. It makes you too vulnerable to being misled or to sharing in the other person's mistakes. I think the Israeli intelligence services are very capable, although their capabilities are at times exaggerated. After all, if we misread the Iraqis in 1990, clearly the Israelis misread the Arabs in October 1973. We all make mistakes in this business.

I think the sharing of information with our friends and allies is very important. It helps us understand each other's perspective, and we all exchange information. It is a mistake to be overly dependent on any one source, but I do not think that is the case in the Middle East. We have good, independent sources of information throughout the region.

QUESTION: Since you raised the issue of the Navy in anti-submarine warfare (ASW), did CIA find out that the Navy was misreading Soviet ASW developments?

MR. GATES: Actually, it ended up being a very cooperative venture with the Navy. The Navy seconded a couple of officers to our effort, made available information that they had gathered, and even made available a couple of submarines to carry out some experiments to see if we could reverse-engineer some things we thought the Soviets were doing. We discovered that the Soviets had made more progress in certain technologies than the Navy had estimated, but that their view of the overall ASW capabilities of the Soviet Navy was approximately correct.

QUESTION: If the original statutory authorization for CIA were to be reviewed today, would any changes be necessary or advisable?

MR. GATES: I think there has been a political evolution in Washington in many areas over the years. Clearly, one has been in the area of congressional oversight and the role of the Congress in overseeing U.S. intelligence operations. If the fundamental statute were to be written from scratch today, I would clean up and consolidate many of the specific actions and practices that have gradually led to the current practice of congressional oversight and make it a fundamental part of the process.

My own view is that congressional oversight is valuable and important. I think it plays a legitimizing role for American intelligence operations and should give the American people confidence that the intelligence system is operating under a set of rules and principles with which at least their representatives are comfortable. Much of the trouble the agency has gotten into over the years, particularly in the early 1960s and the assassination business, involved acts that were directed by presidents. I believe that if there had been congressional oversight during that period, some of those problems would have been avoided.

One of the arguments that has been made against congressional oversight is that Congress is unable to keep a secret. In my view, since at least 1986 the congressional oversight committees have done a better job of protecting intelligence secrets than the executive branch. I am more willing to trust the two intelligence committees of the Congress with some of our sensitive information than I am with a number of people in the executive branch. Unfortunately, I don't have any choice about whom to trust. I traveled to England, where they are attempting to create a system of parliamentary oversight for their intelligence services, and was asked questions like, "Isn't this really dangerous?" We thought the same thing in the mid-1970s when serious congressional oversight began in the United States. I do not believe it has hampered our activities in the slightest. I think, frankly, that while we have been stopped from doing a few things we probably should have been allowed to do, for the most part those activities the Congress curtailed should probably have not been done in the first place. Congress has acted as a useful check on the executive branch.

One of the dangers in covert action is that policymakers fail to see covert action as a useful complement to an overt policy—as a way of enhancing or improving an overt policy. Too often policymakers in the past have turned to covert action as a substitute for policy or because they could not figure out any other way to deal with the problem, even though the prospects for success of the covert action were fairly remote. I think that the congressional oversight process provides a "sanity check" on things of that nature and thus serves a useful purpose.

We need to deal with leaks of intelligence information, however, which is a difficult thing to handle. When we invest billions of dollars in technologies or satellite capabilities or when we send human agents in harm's way to collect information that is desperately needed, it is a terrible waste to have the value of those technical systems invalidated or to have a human agent killed or put at risk because of leaks. We could put in place tougher penalties and tougher measures to deal with leaks if we had a more regularized congressional oversight process. I think many people leak information in the belief that this is the way to get accountability. Sometimes they do it for ego; sometimes they do it because they don't like the policy. I think that a good congressional oversight program would undermine some of those rationales. If I were redoing the legislation, I would include congressional oversight provisions from the beginning.

NARRATOR: The media has criticized President Bush for taking too long to make up his mind about the meaning of the liquidation of the Soviet empire. From where you sat in NSC and from where you were later to view the CIA process, is there any validity in this criticism?

MR. GATES: I think that once we can gain a historical perspective on what happened between 1989 and 1991, the skill with which President Bush, Secretary Baker, and others managed the relationship with the Soviet Union will be seen as a remarkable management of a very delicate process. It made it easier—and in some cases possible—for Gorbachev to carry out some of his domestic reforms, as well as relax dominance over Eastern Europe and hostility with respect to Germany. If someone here at the University of Virginia had written in 1988 that within two years the Berlin Wall would be down, Germany would be reunified as a member of NATO with Soviet acquiescence, and that the Soviet Union would collapse or be close to collapsing, they would have been hauled off to Western State Hospital or someplace similar. The fact is that the world became caught up in an incredible rush of revolutions.

I think President Bush managed that process with a great deal of sensitivity and care, which allowed Gorbachev to keep the troops stationed in Eastern Europe inside their barracks and allowed the events to go forward. Bush kept the NATO alliance together, continued the process of arms control, and, in effect, helped the Soviet Union go gently into the good night. I think the fact that the Russian revolution—that is what it really is—has proceeded so far with so little violence is owed in no small part to the skill that the West and the United States displayed in terms of avoiding alarms to the Soviet army, to the KGB, and others that the whole process was being manipulated by the West to the West's own advantage. There are many indigenous factors at work within Russia itself, but the United States played a critical role.

In view of what has happened, I think the administration showed far more foresight than they were given credit for having, and, frankly, the same is true for the CIA. Every American president since Lyndon Johnson knew that the Soviet Union was in an economic crisis, and the information about the crisis was forwarded to them in detail. They knew that the Soviet Union was vulnerable and that dealing with the economy was a priority of the Soviet leadership. The Agency's forecast of serious trouble ahead for the Soviet Union and the possibility of a coup against Gorbachev led us at the National Security Council to begin—on a close-hold basis—contingency planning for the collapse of the Soviet Union. This prediction took place in the fall of 1989, almost two years before it actually happened. The planning group was headed by Condoleezza

Rice (who is now the provost at Stanford University) and included senior-level representatives from the State and Defense Departments and CIA.

One of the criticisms made against President Bush, ironically, is the same type of criticism now being made against President Clinton—that President Bush stayed with Gorbachev too long and that Clinton is staying with Yeltsin too long. You can only have one president at a time. Gorbachev was the person who was making those positive changes in Eastern Europe, who was collaborating with the United States against Iraq (a former Soviet ally), and who was allowing the unification of Germany. If there is a criticism to be leveled against the Bush administration, it is that we probably waited too long to begin expanding our contacts with other leaders in the Soviet system besides Gorbachev, although Yeltsin did come to the White House for a meeting as early as the summer of 1989. President Clinton is absolutely right to be as supportive as he has been of Yeltsin, although I think we now need to keep the pressure on to encourage a return to democratic practices. Hindsight criticism about staying with one leader or another too long is frankly somewhat artificial and unrealistic, in my opinion.

QUESTION: You mentioned that the United States misread the Iraq situation prior to 1990. How did this happen, given the enormous amount of information available as early as 1988 which indicated that Iraq was a dangerous regime? Also, did the administration foresee the possibility of the Kurdish and Shi'a uprisings after Desert Storm? Press reports suggest that the administration was expecting a military uprising in Iraq. If that is true, did the administration have a specific group in mind for ousting Saddam, or was this a general feeling that after such a disastrous military defeat the military would turn on him?

MR. GATES: No one in the administration had any illusions about the kind of leader Saddam Hussein was or the kind of state Iraq was. If you go back and read the minutes of the NSC meetings, the deputies meetings, and others, there were no misperceptions about the brutality and the aggressiveness of Saddam Hussein. Iraq was a serious and dangerous problem that had to be managed in some way, given Saddam's development of weapons of mass destruction in every category. I think that the intelligence judgment was based on the assumption that Saddam would devote some time to rebuilding Iraq, which had just emerged from a decade-long war with Iran that had cost Iraq between $300 and $350 billion and caused a great deal of destruction that left the country deeply in debt and facing many problems. The general view was not that Saddam was a good guy or that he was going to try to make life better for the average Iraqi citizen, but simply that he would take some time to nurse his wounds and try to restore and improve his military capabilities and perhaps complete those weapons of mass destruction. I don't think there was any illusion about the kind of regime that was ruling in Baghdad. It was just a question of how soon he would launch another aggression, and most analysts thought that Iraq would need more time to prepare. This view was shared by virtually every leader in the Middle East, including the person who knew him best, the emir of Kuwait. King Fahd of Saudi Arabia, King Hussein of Jordan—all the people in the region who had dealt with Saddam Hussein closely over a long period of time—shared the view held by the United States regarding Saddam's intentions.

Recently I spoke with Larry Eagleburger and later with Brent Scowcroft about the Shi‘a and Kurdish uprisings after the war, and it is somewhat disconcerting to discover how much you forget about events that took place not too long ago. My recollection is that in all honesty, there was not much of a forecast of an ethnic uprising in Iraq. There *was* the hope that a military uprising would occur, but I don't think anyone had any concrete information suggesting that there would be one. The general view was that the Shi‘a and Kurdish uprisings may have prevented the very military coup for which we hoped because the Iraqi military was faced with the possibility at the end of the war that Iraq might cease to exist as a unified country. They had a choice of watching the country fall apart through civil war and letting the Shi‘a in the south and the Kurds in the north go their own way, or supporting Saddam Hussein. If those uprisings had not taken place, I personally think that the odds of military action against Saddam would have been higher, but there was no specific expectation of it, as far as I remember.

QUESTION: What prompted the massive U.S. military buildup in the 1980s, which was one of the major contributors to our national debt that we are finally addressing and will have to continue to address for another ten years?

MR. GATES: I think the military buildup resulted from a perception on the part of President Reagan, Congress, and the American people that the Soviets had been racing to build their weapons programs, both strategic and conventional, while the United States had not even been running in that race. One of the lines bandied about was that there was no arms race because only one country was racing. The reality, I think, is not too different from that perception. There was never the belief among the experts that the Soviets had established strategic superiority over the United States. The United States had watched the Soviets go from approximately 150 ICBM launchers in the mid-1960s to more than 1,500 by 1972, however. The United States had 1,054 ICBMs at the end of the 1960s and still had 1,054 at the end of the 1970s. The United States had only two weapons programs that were underway during the 1970s: the placing of multiple independently targeted re-entry vehicles (MIRVs) on a portion of our ICBMs, and the construction of the Trident submarine. Our airmen were flying B-52 bombers that in many instances were older than the pilots themselves.

Meanwhile, we saw the Soviets engaged in modernization of a broad array of their weapons systems. Most worrisome was the MIRVing of the SS-18, their blockbuster ICBM with ten warheads and the capability to carry 14 warheads. The Soviets also were increasing the accuracy of that missile to the point where it would be effective in an attack against our missile silos. Furthermore, the Soviets deployed for the first time a generation of a new strategic bomber, the Blackjack, and two different kinds of mobile ICBMs—one train-mounted and one road-mobile—that made it increasingly difficult for us to put their ICBM force at risk in a context of either deterrence or war fighting.

These developments on the Soviet side, in addition to their continuing construction of a strategic defense infrastructure, led to the willingness of Congress to fund the substantial enhancement of our strategic programs—the 50 MX missiles, the B-1 bomber, the B-2 Stealth bomber (the development of which began in the Carter administration), cruise missiles, and the improved D-5 missile to go with the Trident submarine. I believe that was an honest and appropriate response to the programs the Soviet Union had underway at the signing of SALT II in 1979 and the advent of the Reagan administration.

Returning to the first point I made about continuity, the reality is that the Trident submarine, the MX missile, and the Stealth bomber were all promoted during the Carter administration. Those were weapons systems that President Carter kept alive and pushed. The Soviet threat, therefore, was not just a right-wing Republican perception. It was a bipartisan perception that the Congress agreed to fund to overcome.

QUESTION: Is there a possibility that Americans remain trapped in Vietnamese prisons?

MR. GATES: I don't think that anyone is in a position to say absolutely that there are no live Americans still being kept in Indochina. What I can say is that I know of no instance in which we pursued evidence that led to anything other than the conclusion that the initial reports were inaccurate. We received many reports over the years about live Americans. We would then track down that evidence and try to find those people, either through technical means or through human agents. We were never able to find one.

One of the tragic parts of this whole business is that a fair number of people (including some Americans), who in essence were con men, began operating out of Bangkok and other places. There were many scams in which money changed hands with families and others in the hope that they could find people still in the prisons. I don't know of a single one of these cases that ever came to fruition. It is impossible to close the book on the issue because we don't have perfect information. What I can say is that in every instance of which I am aware where there were indications of a live sighting, we were unable to confirm it.

QUESTION: Mr. Eagleburger, during which years were you ambassador to Yugoslavia and would you update us on your assessment of the situation today in Bosnia-Herzegovina?

MR. EAGLEBURGER: I was ambassador from 1977 to 1981. I left there to come back and become a part of the Reagan administration. My estimate hasn't changed; if anything, I am more pessimistic. I think it is unlikely that they will get a peace settlement, and even if they do get one, it is unlikely that it will hold. In essence, I must say that I think the bad guys have won—the Bosnian Serbs. They are not the only people engaged in ethnic cleansing, but they are the most active and certainly the most successful in it. If there is a peace agreement, there will probably be a rump Bosnian Muslim state, but it is not likely to last very long. I am also inclined to think that it would not be long before all three parties were back at each others' throats trying to change the settlement. In that context, I have raised serious questions about American troops on the ground as part of a peacekeeping operation. I make that statement recognizing that the administration has committed itself, and I think once a commitment is made, it should be carried out. I'm not sure that the situation will ever reach a point where our ground forces are in place, but if it does, we have a serious problem ahead of us.

QUESTION: Mr. Gates, could you discuss the role of the KGB after the collapse of the Soviet Union?

MR. GATES: The Russian KGB, the successor to the Soviet KGB, has significantly reduced its level of activity in many places around the world, particularly in the Third World. It has likewise drawn down and reduced in general terms their level of activity in this country. It is still seeking American technology, however. The theft of technology from the West and particularly the United States had been the Soviet KGB's primary job over the past 10 or 12 years. The Russian KGB is continuing that activity, although with fewer resources than it had before the collapse of the Soviet Union.

By the same token, from looking at the operations of the former Soviet military intelligence service, the GRU, you could not tell that there was ever a revolution. These guys have not diminished the scale of their activity around the world, and in fact, in many places they have increased it and have even become more aggressive. They are also after Western technological secrets, but they are carrying out other activities as well. The military intelligence service seems to be running at a relatively unconstrained level at a time when the KGB has had its resources reduced substantially.

QUESTION: How has Greece—the only member of the European Community and NATO in the region—influenced the Balkan crisis?

MR. GATES: My view is that Greece has not played a significant role up to this point. The Greeks clearly are close to the Serbs. In some limited respects they have probably contributed to evasions of the sanctions by letting supplies through to Serbia. I think, however, that the constituent republics of the former Yugoslavia bear almost the entire blame for what has happened there so far. If the situation were to spread either to Kosovo or to Macedonia, then you might see a more active Greek role.

QUESTION: Does the former Soviet nuclear arsenal pose a threat to the world?

MR. GATES: With the exception of Kazakhstan and Ukraine, all of the nuclear weapons have been consolidated inside Russia. Even before the collapse of the Soviet Union, the Russians worried about ethnic conflict and the volatility of certain regions. Thus, several years ago they began to withdraw nuclear weapons from some of those areas, to put them in safer areas inside Russia, and to enhance their physical security. All of the evidence available to us indicates that the Russians did a comprehensive job and that those weapons are well secured.

My worry, frankly, is not so much that someone might get hold of a loose nuclear weapon or steal one from a storage or deployment site as it is about the fragility of the overall command and control. If the coup against Yeltsin two weeks ago had succeeded, I shudder to think who might now be in possession of the nuclear codes in Russia. That is one of the reasons why I think President Clinton was right to support Yeltsin. I worry about what would happen if Yeltsin disappears from the scene, given the lack of a back bench of democratic leaders who have popular support. They need more time to develop that bench. My worry is less over the physical security of the nuclear weapons than the integrity of the command and control structure in Moscow should something happen to Yeltsin.

NARRATOR: We are grateful to Dr. Gates for giving us the benefit of his experiences with the CIA and the Bush administration. We also thank Secretary Eagleburger, as we have on other occasions, for his participation.

VI

THE QUESTION OF
PRESIDENTIAL DISABILITY

THE BUSH PRESIDENCY AND PRESIDENTIAL DISABILITY*

BURTON J. LEE III, M.D.

NARRATOR: Dr. Burton J. Lee III was physician to the President and the White House from 1989 to 1993. He received his bachelor's degree from Yale University and his M.D. from Columbia University College of Physicians and Surgeons. Before his White House appointment, he was primarily, but not exclusively, associated with the Sloan-Kettering Cancer Center as resident in medicine, fellow of the department of chemotherapy, and clinical associate. Then he ran the lymphoma service. He had close ties with and worked at Bellevue Hospital, Cornell University Medical Center, Memorial Hospital, and Greenwich Hospital, among others.

Dr. Lee has authored or co-authored 131 published articles in distinguished medical journals and is a member of various editorial boards. He was also the editor of the section on lymphoma and leukemia of the *Year Book of Cancer.* He has been a member of the President's Commission on the Human Immunodeficiency Virus Epidemic, the Presidential Drug Advisory Council, and the White House Task Force on Infant Mortality.

We are delighted to welcome Dr. Lee, who has been involved in two areas of interest to the Miller Center: the presidency and presidential disability, and planning within the White House to prepare for unforeseen emergencies.

Presented in a Forum at the Miller Center of Public Affairs on 4 February 1993.

DR. LEE: I recently gained some notoriety for being figuratively thrown out of the White House for not complying with instructions to give President Clinton his allergy shot. More accurately, they let me go because I was trying to collect his medical records for our White House files.

Actually, the allergy-shot episode involved an amusing sequence of events. A poorly identified box arrived at the southwest gate of the White House. Identification on the box indicated only that it originated in Arkansas and was sent by Clinton's allergist with a handwritten address. Otherwise, there was nothing personal or definitive about the box's identification. Such an event was so outside of the norm that the Secret Service stopped the box at the southwest gate and wouldn't allow the material into the White House. They called my office and said that we would have to clear the box before they let it in.

The Secret Service agents were entirely correct in their actions. We examined the material, which was labeled "President Clinton's allergy medicine." I thought, if Saddam Hussein's people had received a package with the instructions, "Give Saddam Hussein one-half cc every two weeks and his allergies will be better," would Saddam have said, "Oh, yes, I'll just roll up my sleeve"? It was preposterous.

In medicine, one constant problem is misidentification of specimens, drugs, blood transfusions, charts, and X-rays. Such classic mistakes are always followed by six lawyers, each of whom is carrying two briefcases and an arraignment. Therefore, it is out of the question to administer medication without absolute, definitive identification.

It should be added that I never had a chance to speak to the President. I had only been there at their request to effect the transition. The Office of the Physician to the President in the White House is mainly filled by military personnel. I was the only political appointee in the operation and, thus, was the only one out of 19 people who left after the transition. I stayed long enough to ensure that those people, all of whom I had hired, would be given a fair chance and that the transition would be handled properly.

I became involved with Twenty-fifth Amendment issues concerning presidential disability through the Miller Center. I worked with Herb Brownell and Birch Bayh, the architects of the original Twenty-fifth Amendment. Birch Bayh is an extraordinary person, and it was a great pleasure for me to get to know him. At one point, he was a candidate for the presidency of the United States. After talking with him at great length, I came to my own private opinion that if he had ever been elected, he would have been a marvelous president. Herb Brownell is also a most impressive person, but I saw him only once or twice.

In the Bush presidency, we followed the architects' intent of the Twenty-fifth Amendment. Soon after Bush took office, I met with him; the vice president; the chief of staff; the head of the military office; C. Boyden Gray, the legal counsel; and J. Bonnie Newman, who headed the White House. The head of the White House is a big job. Newman coordinated everything related to the White House: Air Force One, the helicopter squadron, Camp David, Kennebunkport, and so forth. We discussed how we wanted issues of presidential disability organized and came to a common understanding of where we were going with it. We decided that the point man would be the chief of staff, and he would make the arrangements. The counsel would draw up the requisite documents. Vice President Quayle knew exactly where he stood, and the President agreed completely with everything that we proposed at that meeting.

Historically, the medical office has never had any clout. At some points, however, individual physicians have had terrific clout. For example, Woodrow Wilson's doctor had clout and apparently ran the country for a while with Mrs. Wilson. Still, in most prior administrations, my position was generally shunted to the background and consulted after the fact. No one put much credence in what came out of the Physician to the President's Office.

At that meeting, I wanted to establish that I or someone whom I had designated in my absence would determine when the President was disabled, and that it would not happen unless I was involved with the decision. A responsible physician taking this duty seriously creates favorable advantages for all of the parties involved. In general, these types of decisions are made by politicians behind closed doors, and the public doesn't get a fair view of what is happening. The Wilson case provides an excellent example, but the public has been dealt with dishonestly by many presidents.

From the medical profession's viewpoint, I also wanted to elevate this office and give it some dignity. In the past, physicians have been pushed around and treated simply as part of the staff.

Throughout this process, I kept in touch with the Miller Center. It has been enormously helpful, and I have taken advice from the Center. I also returned a second time to report on my activities.

We followed the advice of the architects of the Twenty-fifth Amendment, the Miller Center, and the various critics, and it went very satisfactorily. I have read all of the related documents that were sent to the presidential library. I'm grateful that an academically responsible group such as the Miller Center has taken an interest in documenting these details, because history will be thankful.

Presently, there is a dramatic slippage back to what we were trying to avoid in 1989. There is no one to head the medical office, and no one is paying attention to anyone that is there. In the next three to four months, Clinton will probably lose 70 percent of the staff in that office, and no one is on the horizon to take over.

In addition to having an agreed-upon procedure for the transfer of power in cases of presidential disability, it is also important that the president's physician be someone he trusts and who can handle the freight that accompanies the position. Bush's fibrillation and the thyroid episode are cases in point. Graves' disease has a sophisticated biological background. It is not a simple problem and can't be handled in cookbook fashion. The Bushes' case was extraordinarily interesting because they both developed Graves' disease within approximately a year of moving to the White House, which seemed rather remarkable. We did a great deal of epidemiologic work, however, which showed that this is not as rare as we had thought.

The Bush case became more complicated when their dog came down with lupus. Lupus is a connective tissue disease that can be lumped into the same autoimmune category as Graves' disease. I announced that we were going to explore this, and most of the doctors in the country wrote to tell me that I didn't know what I was doing. This happens daily in the White House—you receive a tremendous amount of gratuitous advice. Interestingly, I also received dozens of letters from people who had Graves' disease and whose dog had developed lupus. Unfortunately, it remains a possibility that what the Bushes have is contagious. There are viruses that cause these autoimmune diseases, and they do occur in clusters.

The initial assessment of George Bush's tachycardia and atrial fibrillation indicated that it was not a pro forma event. In this type of case, you don't want a doctor who can't pull the information together properly. After the President had fibrillated, there was an avalanche of advice that questioned why I waited to defibrillate him. Critics felt it was dangerous to have let the President fibrillate and that he should have been electrically defibrillated. Thankfully, we did not electrically defibrillate the President, because that would certainly not have been the way to treat a person with hyperthyroidism. About 12 hours later, we got the correct diagnosis and then began treatment.

We brought in five consultants to deal with the cardiology and thyroid problems from such places as the Mayo Clinic and Johns Hopkins. The best thyroid expert, Ken Burman, actually was working nearby at Walter Reed Hospital, and he ended up managing both Barbara's and George's cases. Then we brought the consultants before the press twice for any and all inquiries that the press might have. I let the consultants handle the technical questions related to their areas of expertise so there would be no question of the fact that they were handling these particular problems instead of me. There are certain areas in which I am an expert and other areas where I am not. I made sure that every time a problem was even slightly out of my area, the best possible person handled it.

This illustrates the necessity of having a presidential physician with academic and clinical skills who has a background in dealing with VIPs. My experience with Clinton is a good example of what happens in VIP medicine. Doctors tend to be fearful and want to please VIPs and chairmen of the board. They want to keep them as patients and don't want to be fired, as I was. They want to remain on the scene, so they cut corners and do what that person asks. This practice is extremely common and it is the main reason why VIPs tend to receive borderline care.

Another reason is that their care tends to be run by committees and not by one person. If anything happens to the plumbing in your house, you want one person in whom you have confidence to be in charge of fixing that plumbing. If he wants a specialist to do a certain job, fine. You want one good person in charge, however. It is dangerous to do anything by committee, especially to run medicine by committee. You need to have someone in charge.

Another episode that demonstrates the importance of having one experienced, responsible person in charge came during Bush's trip to Tokyo. Under no circumstances would I have expected that Bush's illness would cause as much pandemonium as it did, since it was minor. Thousands of people, however, were screaming and yelling while trying to break down doors. The press went completely insane because it looked as if the President had died on television. All of the streets suddenly became impassable. The huge dinner we were attending turned upside down in a second.

There was a U-shaped table, and I was sitting on the inside, halfway down the U. The President was sitting with Prime Minister Kiichi Miyazawa at the head of the table on the outside of the U. I knew that Bush was sick. I had tried to persuade him not to attend, but the dinner with Miyazawa was the primary motivation behind his 12-day Asia trip. He had already gotten sick once, and I told him he wouldn't make it through dinner. Bush felt that he could and had to attend. He is a very strong person, so I told him to try. I watched him periodically throughout the dinner. Suddenly, his face went white, and then green. I tried to reach him from the outside to see if I could do something to get him out of there before anything drastic happened. He went down, however, before I could even get out of the U.

The room became an enormous maelstrom, and I went under the table to attend to Bush. I could see instantly that he was OK. The problem was to clean him up and waste a little time while the Secret Service set up the exit. The head of the Secret Service detail, Rick Miller, was at my left shoulder and did a fantastic job, as did his entire detail. One agent, George Robinson, ran across the top of the table in order to get to Bush, and never spilled a glass! They had to get the cars in place and get a clean coat that we could put over Bush. We wanted him to walk out, not get carried out. There was a great deal of pressure on the medical personnel who accompanied me. They felt Bush should go to the hospital, but I did not want to take him there.

We were dealing with these things while under the table. The President and I were talking, and my nurse suggested that I loosen his belt so he could breathe properly. I agreed and started playing around with his belt and loosened it a little bit. The President's head snapped off the rug and he said, "Burt, what are you doing down there?" At that point, Barbara was watching above us, and when she saw everyone laughing under the table, she took over and gave her great performance that saved the day.

Those situations will happen, and the Secret Service is terribly thankful if there is a doctor on the scene who can manage the crisis properly. Historically, more often than not the Secret Service has managed such situations, because they have not been completely sure that the doctor has correctly interpreted the situation.

I would like to discuss the constitutional issues that involve presidential disability. Should civilians run the medical office? Historically, a military person has frequently managed it. I don't want to exaggerate, but generals and admirals typically do not make the best clinicians. They normally have occupied administrative positions in the military for some time and haven't worked much in the active clinical care of patients. In contrast, when I joined the administration, I came from a huge practice in New York. My background was clinical.

There are some merits in having a military person run the office in that everything can be kept within a tight military framework. Generally, the head of the White House military office, the head of the White House itself, or the chief of staff would supervise the chief of the medical office. For instance, when I refused to give the injection to Clinton, it was promptly given thereafter by one of my other physicians, a Navy doctor who has no legitimate way to say no. There is a great deal of heat and light in that White House on everything that happens, and the doctor ended up not handling the pressure too well.

As a civilian head of the medical office, I was able to operate independently. If I needed someone from Walter Reed, I took someone from Walter Reed. If I needed someone from Bethesda, I took someone from Bethesda. If I needed someone from New York, I got someone from New York, and so forth. Bob Waller of the Mayo Clinic, for instance, was the best eye specialist I could have had for Mrs. Bush's Graves' disease. As a civilian, I had the independence and ability to say no.

The presidential physician will probably be a friend of the president in some way as well, which is important, because unquestionably you have to have that person's trust. Nancy Reagan never trusted any of her husband's doctors, and they all suffered some bad side effects from that distrust. Ultimately, she called in outside people to examine her husband, for example. The confusion about who was in charge was clearly present both when Ronald Reagan was shot and when he received treatment for his colon cancer. That wasn't the doctors' fault as much as it was the fault of the person who appointed the physician in charge. Although that physician was appointed, apparently he did not carry the faith and trust of the first couple. All of the doctors were constantly undermined. It is difficult to care for someone without having their trust.

I also would like to discuss my view of the job of being the president's physician. The way it is currently structured, it is a terrible job. You need everyone's goodwill to make anything of it. Also, for a physician who is accustomed to dealing at a certain level, it is almost a servile job. It never even occurs to anyone to ask your opinion about anything other than personal medical problems. I object strenuously to that. As the job is currently structured, I would not advise any senior person to take it without being fully aware that they will be one of the household help for a while.

When I first accepted the job, Bush spoke to me in December 1988. He wanted to compress the White House staff and eliminate some positions. He asked me to run the White House medical unit and to be the special assistant to the president for health care policy. Between that discussion and arriving in Washington, I lost the health-policy job. John Sununu, the chief of staff, wanted a strongly conservative staff that shared his conservative views. He probably made a smart move, because I disagreed with him on almost everything. While my friends in New York think I'm a rabid conservative, in Washington I became known as the "White House Communist."

The weekend before I moved to Washington, Andrew Card, Sununu's assistant, told me the bad news. I have never met a nicer person than Andy Card. For the record, this is a person who handled a tremendous amount of dirty work for Sununu, yet I don't think he made an enemy in the White House. After Card's phone call, I deliberated all weekend, but I finally decided that I would take this job and try to see what I could do. I was not successful, however, and they kept me almost completely out of the decision-making process.

I wouldn't recommend this particular job to anyone of prominence without something else to go along with it. Most people get into the White House and get an ego boost. I went into the White House and almost had my ego destroyed because of the nature of this job—you spend most of your time waiting in holding rooms and standing in the background. My main reason for accepting the position was that it gave me an opportunity to get involved with the health care-delivery question—what everyone is discussing today. That is what I wanted our administration to deal with. In my first visit with Governor Sununu I said we had to address this health care-delivery question. America needs it, and the access-versus-cost equation with which Clinton is now wrestling is terribly important. I said that if we didn't do it, sooner or later someone else would. Fifteen percent of Americans have no access to the system, and I feel that it is physicians' moral duty as a profession to help handle this problem. It is objectionable to me that politicians seem to run in and handle it because we won't. I told Sununu that if Bush weren't reelected, someone else would run in and do it, and we might not like the results. I argued that even if we didn't get it through Congress, we would at least get our foot in the door and establish a position on this issue. I couldn't convince anyone to address health care until Harris Wofford won in Pennsylvania. When Wofford defeated Dick Thornburgh in Pennsylvania, the whole White House suddenly said, "We have to approach the health care issue." I want doctors to be in on the decision-making process, and they certainly are not at the present time.

QUESTION: It seems to me that the Twenty-fifth Amendment has the unfortunate result, if actually used as written, of setting up a regency in which the regent becomes president until the president decides to resume the presidency. The regent will, I think, be timid because he doesn't know whether the president would approve of what he did or didn't do. For that reason, I think the amendment could be viewed as an elaborate attempt to provide a legalistic solution to a crisis situation that had previously been handled haphazardly. Either the president could function or he couldn't. The logic of the Constitution before the amendment was added was that either the president would recover quickly or could resign. I don't have any solution to this dilemma. Could you comment on the regency issue?

DR. LEE: The fact that this person is a regent is not all bad. I understand your point, but if I were the president, I would want the vice president to act in a way that I would tend to agree with when I resumed control. I would try to ensure that the person who was taking over would do certain things. Similarly, a CEO wouldn't turn his company over to someone who was antithetical to his point of view while he took a vacation.

A difficult situation in the White House, which happened with Eisenhower, Nixon, Kennedy, and Johnson, exists when the president and others actually dislike the vice president. It creates an attitude in the White House of, "We are never going to turn control over to this person." Even Bush could have been under anesthesia at some point if we had electrically defibrillated him. Therefore, I don't find that the idea of a regent in the Twenty-fifth Amendment is bad.

QUESTION: Most of the cases you have discussed require the president to be aware of his illness and willing to be treated. In the psychiatric field, though, that is often not the case. Lincoln's depression, Andrew Johnson's alcoholism, Secretary James Forrestal's attempt to conceal his illness, which led ultimately to his suicide, all raise the issue of presidential psychological disability. Under the Twenty-fifth Amendment or other proposed procedures, what will be done the next time we have a president with some kind of mental illness?

DR. LEE: That is a surprisingly common problem. Lyndon Johnson almost certainly was a manic-depressive. He suffered long periods of depression, but when he was up, get out of his way! At the second Miller Center meeting, I agreed that mental illness would be my toughest problem as the president's physician. This raised the issue of whether we should have psychiatrists on call. I felt that psychiatrists should not be on call. If there is a mental illness, however, the president's physician must choose the right psychiatrist to see the president.

One factor that helped my particular tenure is that Barbara Bush is a very stable person who does not seek the limelight. There is nothing frivolous about the woman. She does not stargaze in the White House; rather, she has her feet on the ground. My greatest ally, if we had encountered a serious mental-illness problem, would have been Mrs. Bush. The children, whom I know very well, would also have been allies. The oldest son, George, for instance, has a tremendous, beneficial influence on his father. The President also listened to Marvin carefully. He listens to all of his children. Even in normal life, mental illness is unbelievably difficult to handle. Nevertheless, it would be another virtue to have a close friend involved with the treatment.

QUESTION: How do you balance between the public's right to know about the president's health and the confidentiality on which any physician-patient relationship centers?

DR. LEE: Marlin Fitzwater asked me how to respond to questions about the public's right to know and privacy. I told him that the public has a right to know about the physical or mental incapacity of a figure who might be elected to any public office. I don't like the word *right*, but it seems to me that the public has every reason to believe that this particular person will be honest about his or her health. If the doctor releases information on the president's or an elected official's health, the public should have every reason to believe that the information is true.

On the other hand, I think historically that the press has every reason to believe that it should maintain a healthy skepticism about such information because there are, of course, many things a physician or candidate doesn't tell. Does the public want to know everything that happens medically to the first lady and the president during four years? Of course not. They will want to know the pertinent issues, and it is the physician's job to dissect out those pertinent issues and put them on the table. There will be, as there were during my tenure, many small, unimportant things that aren't announced. The decision to release medical information lies with the physician and the president. I won't say anything that President Bush doesn't say or that he doesn't approve. President Bush and I acted in concert; there was no difficulty about that.

The Paul Tsongas case, however, illustrates the issue well. If you have any kind of recurrence of lymphoma after a marrow transplant, that person is not cured. Tsongas had a recurrence, but somehow that was kept from the public. I don't know who was responsible for the lack of disclosure. Tsongas, in his latest report, seemed to indicate that it was someone in his press office. Nevertheless, it was a serious omission.

With the Tsongas case, I think there was the additional problem of press bias. I gave interviews on his lymphoma, for instance, to the Associated Press and the *New York Times*. Indisputably, we are a long way from being able to claim that we can cure nodular or indolent lymphoma with marrow transplants. Tsongas and his doctor know this. Nothing that I said in those interviews was ever printed, however.

After Larry Altman wrote an article in the *New York Times* about Clinton's health, I received many phone calls. I told Helen Thomas at great length what was omitted from the Altman report. A great deal was omitted. If I had been a medical correspondent, I could have thought of 20 pertinent questions concerning information that had been omitted. Helen Thomas may have written an article on this, but again, her editors published nothing. This is a small comment on press bias, which was severe in 1992.

QUESTION: In the latter part of President Nixon's term, his chief of staff, Alexander Haig, said that because Nixon was drunk much of the time, Haig himself conducted the office business. This apparently was in the period just before Nixon resigned. In a case like that, would the presidential physician know or be involved?

DR. LEE: I would have to assume that the presidential physician would know. I was unaware that this was a real problem for Nixon. This is the first time I have ever heard that. Alcoholism goes under the rubric of mental illness and is a tough problem to handle. Nixon was certainly under a great deal of strain.

QUESTION: When President Reagan had surgery for cancer, I believe he just passed a note on to Vice President Bush. Afterward, he underwent quite a bit of sedation for a period of maybe a week or ten days. Were they circumventing the Twenty-fifth Amendment?

DR. LEE: No, I think Dan Ruge said later that they hadn't actually thought about the Twenty-fifth Amendment after the assassination attempt, but it was put into effect prior to Reagan's cancer surgery.

If something happened now to Clinton, it is uncertain what they would do, as I mentioned before.

QUESTION: Is the Twenty-fifth Amendment only good for long-term illness?

DR. LEE: No, we would have exercised it if we had anesthetized the President for five minutes, which we might have done at one point for defibrillation. I think Dan Ruge's experience is attributable to the lack of authority that he was given in the job, which was mainly due to Mrs. Reagan. She was managing things, and even the chief of staff realized that if he had a tricky problem, the first person with whom he should check was Nancy Reagan. On medical matters, if you have to go through that kind of process, you quickly run into a great deal of difficulty.

NARRATOR: Reagan said that he never met with the vice president until the day after the assassination attempt. He had no contact, yet that relationship is critical, isn't it?

DR. LEE: It is very critical, and it's interesting that during the eight years the Reagans were in the White House, I have been reliably told that the Bushes were never once invited as a couple to dine, have a drink, or do anything with the Reagans on the second floor of the White House. George Bush went up there two or three times to see Reagan on administrative and presidential matters. I believe, however, that Barbara Bush was never invited to the second floor, and as a couple, they were never invited by the Reagans to their 2nd floor White House home. I think that the Bushes are saints for how generous they have been in their treatment of the Reagans. I'm not that big a person. Even a casual observer could spot the difficulties that existed between those two couples.

Still, Ronald Reagan, personally, was a generous person, and he acted quickly once the Twenty-fifth Amendment issue was raised. He quickly turned responsibility over to George Bush, and I think in many ways he became close to George Bush. Socially, however, the couples never interacted.

QUESTION: What is your perception of the Office of the Physician to the President, particularly with regard to the military? How do you perceive the evolution of the White House physician and this interrelationship between the military and civilian medicine?

DR. LEE: When I was there, I made every effort to have extremely good relationships with the military personnel. During my first month, I had all of the various surgeons general over for lunch at the White House with their people who were on my staff. At one point, I even went to see the secretary of the Navy because I thought that they should be handling their physicians differently. There is always a struggle in the Navy between line officers and the physicians, because the line officers want the doctors out on the ships. In today's medicine, it is unnecessary to station a doctor on every submarine, destroyer, tanker, and so forth. Medical emergencies can be handled beautifully by independent duty corpsmen, physician assistants, nurse practitioners, and on-shore consultants in light of modern telecommunications and transportation.

I invested a great deal of effort in having a close relationship with the military. Admiral Don Hagen, the head of Bethesda Naval Hospital for three of the years that I was there, is now surgeon general of the Navy. He did a marvelous job, and we became good friends. It is important for a civilian physician to operate closely with the military for innumerable reasons. The facilities at Walter Reed and Bethesda are unparalleled for taking care of a president. There is nothing like them in any civilian hospital in the country.

In contrast, caring for Reagan at the George Washington hospital disrupted patient care throughout that entire hospital and made the management of his case incredibly difficult. There were reporters running up and down the back service elevators, bribing food service personnel, and placing microphones all over the place. The situation was completely out of control.

A civilian can choose which facilities are best to treat the president. A military physician may feel bound by service loyalty to place the president in a particular hospital.

NARRATOR: We have had the benefit of a wise and carefully thought-through perspective on many aspects of this question. We are grateful to Dr. Lee for continuing his relationship with the Miller Center.

ADDENDUM—JUNE 20, 1993

Since the above interview, I have learned that President Clinton has adopted our plan for the Twenty-fifth Amendment (the Bush plan) in its entirety. The missing pieces are that a physician to the President has yet to be appointed, the presidential medical records are still not in the White House, and Clinton apparently still is undecided about using the military medicine system (a serious mistake, in my view).

Dr. Burton J. Lee

VII

THE 1992 ELECTION

CHAPTER 10

HOW GEORGE BUSH LOST THE PRESIDENTIAL ELECTION IN 1992[*]

BETTY GLAD

NARRATOR: One of the most popular books ever published by the Miller Center was a book entitled *Lessons from Defeated Presidential Candidates*. One of the contributors was Professor Betty Glad, who wrote the chapter on Charles Evans Hughes.

Betty Glad is a professor in the Department of Government and International Affairs at the University of South Carolina. She is currently president of the International Society for Political Psychology and has also been president of the American Political Science Association Presidency Research Group.

Professor Glad is the author of a large number of books, including *Jimmy Carter: In Search of the Great White House* (1980), *Charles Evans Hughes and the Illusions of Innocence: A Study in American Diplomacy* (1966), *Key Pittman: The Tragedy of a Senate Insider* (1986), editor of *The Psychological Dimensions of War* (1990), and editor of *The Role of the Public in the Formulation of U.S. Foreign Policy* (1966).

Today she takes on the challenging subject of how George Bush lost the presidential election in 1992. We have had some 25 people in the Bush oral history series, and almost every one of them has asked that same question. Former Miller Center Council member Charles Bartlett thinks it is one of the great mysteries of

---

[*]*Presented in a Forum at the Miller Center of Public Affairs on 23 June 1994.*

U.S. presidential election history. We are delighted that she could return and speak on President Bush.

MS. GLAD: In talking about Bush, I feel more trepidation than I did about Charles Evans Hughes because the full record and medical records are not yet available. What I will say is simply a first attempt to explain what happened in the 1992 election.

At the beginning of the 1992 campaign, George Bush had several advantages over his potential Democratic competitors. He was strong in the polls. Following the war against Iraq, he had an 89 to 90 percent approval rating in most of the surveys. As a consequence, the major potential Democratic contenders—Jay Rockefeller and Mario Cuomo, for example—decided not to run.

Of the second-tier candidates, two quickly surfaced as the front-runners—former Massachusetts Senator Paul Tsongas and Arkansas Governor Bill Clinton. Both of these individuals had serious vulnerabilities. Tsongas clearly had a health problem, and he lacked charisma. In fact, he was very similar to failed Democratic presidential candidate Michael Dukakis in terms of the campaign rhetoric he used.

Bill Clinton also had some vulnerabilities. He was from the small state of Arkansas, and most people were unfamiliar with his record. Furthermore, a character issue surfaced around the time of the New Hampshire primary, when Gennifer Flowers went to the mass media and accused Clinton of marital infidelity. The draft issue also surfaced at this time. Clinton therefore seemed very vulnerable on personal grounds and also appeared to lack an overwhelming political record that would override these vulnerabilities.

President Bush, partly as a consequence of these considerations, relied on strategies that had worked for Republicans in the past. First, he conducted an Oval Office strategy. Whether by choice or by temperament, he decided to run on his record. He also stayed in the White House. His aides attempted to get him to campaign, but he really only hit the campaign trail in the early primary season and at the end of the general election in the fall. He left most of the campaigning to other Republicans. Bush also emphasized his foreign policy successes such as the military victories in Panama and in Iraq against Saddam Hussein. In the domestic sphere, he focused on such accomplishments as the Clean Air Act and the Americans with Disabilities Act. He downplayed the economy, however, and generally discussed it as little as possible.

Second, Bush and Vice President Dan Quayle moved politically to the Right in an effort to consolidate his standing with the most conservative wing of the Republican party. The right-wing had always been suspicious of Bush because he did not have his origins in that section of the party. Before the 1980 campaign, he had been a member of the Council on Foreign Relations, the Trilateral Commission, and other "suspect groups", at least from the viewpoint of the radical Right. He also was against a constitutional amendment to negate *Roe v. Wade* at that time.

To allay right-wing suspicions based on his political past, George Bush made it clear at the beginning of the 1992 campaign that he was not going to replace Dan Quayle as his running mate, even though people were raising issues about Quayle because of Bush's health problems. He also began to emphasize traditional family values in his rhetoric. Finally, and perhaps most importantly, Bush allowed Patrick Buchanan and other members of the party's radical Right to have prime-time T.V. exposure at the 1992 Republican National Convention. As a result, the radical Right seemed to many people to be dominating the Republican message at the convention.

Finally, near the end of the campaign, when the polls were making him nervous, George Bush's campaign took a negative turn. He not only critiqued the record of his opponent, which is certainly what one is supposed to do in a campaign, he also became very personal. He compared Clinton's foreign policy experience with that of his dog, Millie. On 7 October on "Larry King Live," in a set of carefully guarded innuendoes, Bush even suggested that Clinton might have engaged in disloyal acts when he traveled to the Soviet Union while a student at Oxford. He thought it strange that Clinton went to Moscow one year after the Soviets crushed Czechoslovakia and did not remember whom he saw. He wondered how Clinton could remember whom he saw in the airport at Oslo but could not remember what he saw in the airport at Moscow.

In this particular election season, Bush's negative campaigning did not work, and there was a precipitous decline in his popularity. By December 1991, his favorable ratings fell to 47 percent. On the eve of the Republican National Convention, he had the lowest favorable rating of any president at a comparable point. In the general election, Bush garnered only 37.7 percent of the popular vote to Clinton's 43.2 percent and Ross Perot's 19 percent. The electoral college vote was 370 to 168 against him. He also lost several states that had voted mainly Republican in recent years—Vermont, New York, California, Illinois, New Jersey, among others. To explain Bush's loss in the 1992 election, I will look at the structural factors over which Bush had no control and the ideological and strategic choices in areas where he had some latitude.

Five structural factors contributed to Bush's loss. First, foreign policy was no longer a Republican issue. With the Soviet Union gone and the Cold War over, people were less interested in foreign policy. U.S. victories against Panama and Iraq were not the most salient issue for the American public. Second, the economy appeared to be getting worse. Trend lines were important. In April 1992, the unemployment rate was 7.2 percent, but in May it was 7.5 percent. Polls showed that voters during this election were also not interested in family values. Rather, they were interested in the economy and wanted economic issues to be addressed by the candidates.

Third, the entrance of Patrick Buchanan into the Republican primary campaign hurt Bush. Buchanan's contention that Bush was less trustworthy than Ted Kennedy seriously undermined Bush's credibility. Fourth, Ross Perot's independent campaign reinforced Clinton's message. Like Clinton, Perot argued that the economy was the major issue. Perot's withdrawal from the campaign just prior to the Democratic National Convention, and his assertion that the Democrats seemed to have their act together also reinforced the Clinton candidacy.

Fifth, and most important, the Democratic nominee in 1992 ran a smart campaign. Bill Clinton understood that the important campaign messages come through the mass media and that they must be shaped and framed. It is not sufficient to run on one's own record. Thus, Clinton was very good at theme management. He took an enormous beating in January and February on the character issue, but he managed to come back, win the Super-Tuesday primaries in the South, and become the front-runner. He cultivated an image as the "comeback kid"—a man with tenacity who could not be beaten and who was the kind of person America needed as president.

This impression worked for awhile, but then the Clinton people discovered shortly before the convention that he was having serious problems in the polls. In their so-called Manhattan project, the Clinton team experimented with a series of themes, testing them with a variety of different focus groups. They discovered that something in Clinton's background worked in his favor, but it was something about which Bill Clinton was apprehensive and a little ashamed. Clinton had come from a relatively humble family in which the father had been an alcoholic and had abused his wife. With this information, people began to feel sympathetic and to understand him. The result was a new theme at the convention: Bill Clinton was now the "Man from Hope."

The Clinton campaign also discovered alternative ways of getting on television. Clinton made 47 appearances on talk shows, as opposed to Perot's 33 and George Bush's 16. Talk shows give people the feeling that they know the candidate and have an intimate tie and personal relationship with the man.

The Clinton campaign staff also saw the need to answer the Bush campaign's negative charges immediately. They would try to respond in the same news cycle. The goal was to preempt the story from appearing altogether or to at least ensure that the media carried the rebuttal from the Clinton people. The Clinton team also counterattacked. For example, in the first presidential campaign debate in St. Louis in October, Clinton used George Bush's father against him. Clinton said, "When Joe McCarthy went around this country attacking people's patriotism, he was wrong, and a senator from Connecticut named Prescott Bush stood up to him. Your father was right to stand up to Joe McCarthy. You were wrong to attack my patriotism. I was opposed to the war, but I loved my country."

Still, there were factors over which Bush had more control, and in these areas he made several ideological, tactical, and stylistic mistakes. Bush was an economic conservative who did not really want new governmental programs. When the representatives from the media asked what his new economic program was, Bush was stymied ideologically. He simply did not believe in initiating a lot of new economic programs, and he would have been untrue to himself had he done so. He could have attempted to explain why his conservative philosophy would work, urged people to be patient, and provided what some commentators have called "reassurance politics." He didn't say those things, however. He just overlooked them, and that oversight was a mistake.

Tactically, he overcorrected to the Right. Patrick Buchanan never had more than about 30 percent popular support during the primary campaigns. Moreover, most of the polls showed that people were voting for Buchanan simply to send a message to George Bush. Sometimes that message was a mixed one. Sometimes, they wanted him to do something about the economy. Sometimes people just wanted to convey the betrayal they felt because of Bush's tax increase during the 1990 budget compromise. Furthermore, at the Republican National Convention, still others—the country club Republicans, independents, and so-called Reagan Democrats who may have voted for Bush—did not like his right-wing rhetoric. A surge of support came after the convention, but it was not the usual increase that one expects after such an event. This small surge quickly spiraled downward.

Stylistically, George Bush demonstrated a strange passivity during the campaign. His failure to defend his economic record suggests that he really did not care about the issue. For example, before the New Hampshire primary, the voters in that state were very concerned about the economy. Bush told them to wait for his State of the Union Address; but when he gave that speech, the first half of it was devoted to foreign policy. Though the second part of the speech focused on what he had done for the economy during his presidency, he gave no explanation of why the economy would get better during a second Bush term.

Bush appeared complacent in other ways. When asked earlier by *Newsweek* correspondent Margaret Garrard Warner why he had entered politics, he said, "It's hard to describe. I got intrigued with it; I felt fascinated, believe in the country, in its strength, in helping people. You know, all of the reasons people go into politics. Challenges and rewards." Even more damaging was his response to a question at the Richmond debate in the fall when a member of the audience asked how the national debt had influenced each candidate's life. Bush responded by mentioning its effect on the interest rates. He said that he loved his grandchildren and wanted to think that they would be able to afford an education and so on. He did not really address the concerns and feelings of the people. He said he knew about the poor, but when he was pushed on this issue, he said he had been at a church and read something on the bulletin board. Apparently, he did not know anyone personally who was hurting, and that is the important point.

Bush's rhetoric also had a rather eccentric quality. He was really a New England aristocrat, but he felt he had to play the "good ol' boy" on the campaign. It sounded false and resulted in a series of nonsequiturs. After one of his health scares, he was asked if he was going to replace Quayle on the 1992 ticket. His response was, "Do you want that by hand or do you want that by word?" whatever that meant. In Dover, New Hampshire, he explained that despite his burdens, he felt blessed. "Don't cry for me, Argentina," he said. He called Gore the "Ozone Man," saying, "This guy is so far off in the environmental extreme we'll be up to our necks in owls and out of work for every American. This guy's crazy. He's way out, far out. Far out, man!" At a rally in Wisconsin during Halloween, Bush warned that if Clinton were elected, every day would be Halloween—fright, terror, and witches everywhere.

The rhetoric did not match the man and his background, so he came off in a sense as not being genuine in the campaign. Political analyst Sidney Blumenthal said: "He walked like a patrician; he looked like a patrician; he had the accents of a patrician; yet he did not really talk like one. The purpose of the use of the vernacular by the genteel is always an effort to cover a vast social distance." George Bush had the social distance, but he did not cover it by the use of this kind of language.

This kind of rhetorical overinvolvement comes from a lack of ability to intuit what is happening in a scene, what people are thinking, and how they are feeling. This lack is evident in George Bush's handling of the wimp charge earlier in his career. He had to look tough, so he manufactured toughness. For example, in the 1984 vice-presidential campaign, he debated Geraldine Ferraro and said afterwards that "he really beat ass" in that debate. That is not what a "good ol' boy" says about a debate with a woman. As commentators note, he seemed to have a manufactured anger. It didn't seem to be genuine or coming from his inner core.

Bush's tactical and stylistic errors were a reflection of his difficulty in finding new paths to deal with the problems he faced. He was at his best when he was following a route that could be understood in terms of traditional values and ways of doing things. The energy he showed, for example, in putting together the alliance against Iraq was the consequence of his knowledge that he was right. He had heard Henry Stimson speak about the need to stand up to dictators when he was at Phillips Academy in Andover, and it impressed him deeply. Bush now relied on the Munich metaphor and the Hitler analogy. He was forming a coalition against an aggressor, thinking that if Saddam Hussein were not stopped in Kuwait, he might do something worse later.

It was not clear to anyone, however, just what should be done about the economy in 1992. What does one do about a $4 trillion debt? What should be done in an economy where major firms are downsizing and jobs are being lost by middle class people and skilled workers? No one knew for sure, and Bush did not have the ability to find an answer for these problems.

Bush's hyperactivity as president can also be understood in terms of his difficulties in setting a domestic political course. He did too much in too little time, resembling a windmill at times. He appeared flustered and lacking in direction. When he was first in office, this hyperactivity was seen as an indication that Bush was going to be a hands-on leader, but he soon seemed to lack direction. As early as March 1989, journalist Lesley Stahl already saw signs of a failed presidency and said that this president didn't know what he was doing or where he was going. That observation is partly the result of too many messages coming out. Bush did not control the situation and direct things to the extent he should have.

At the most basic level, George Bush was an organization man. Author William Whyte, Jr., observed some time ago the widespread phenomenon of individuals who get their security from working within an organizational framework. They are people who are characterized by going along and who display loyalty and hard work, but essentially direction is provided to them by the top man or by the organization itself. Let us turn to George Bush's early career to see his development along these lines.

John Byrnes, the ranking Republican on the House Ways and Means Committee, noted that as a member of Congress Bush was a nice-guy, was hard-working, and always did what was expected of him. As U.N. ambassador from 1971 to 1973, he forcefully supported what he saw as the U.S. two-Chinas policy at the same time that Henry Kissinger was undercutting him in negotiations with the PRC. Bush, however, did not become angry when he discovered what Kissinger was doing. As chair of the Republican National

Committee from 1973 to 1974, Bush was completely loyal to
President Nixon. In fact, he was one of the last people to urge
Nixon to resign and waited until the House Judiciary Committee
began moving towards a vote to do so.

As chief of the U.S. Liaison Office to Peking, Bush was not a
policymaker. Nevertheless, he chose the Peking post, even though
he was told that Kissinger would be making policy. As director of
the CIA, Bush built morale and made people in the agency feel
better about themselves. In dealing with the Soviet estimates,
however, he hedged when presented with the in-house Committee
A Report and the outside Committee B Report. Both insiders and
outsiders said they never knew which he considered the most
accurate assessment.

As vice president, Bush took few visible stands as the memoirs
of the Reagan administration officials suggest. Bush says that he
kept his advice for Reagan private; but he certainly never entered
into the discussions and intellectual battles in which other members
of the administration participated. Bush's caution was clearly
evident after the attempt on Reagan's life. Aides suggested that
Bush take a helicopter directly to the White House, but Bush
declined, saying it would be very bad imagery for the vice president
to go to the White House in a helicopter as if he were president.
Instead, he opted to be taken to the vice presidential mansion and
then go by automobile to the White House.

This caution was rooted in George Bush's temperament and
early life experiences. He was very sociable as a young boy and
wanted to be liked. He was very attached to his older brother,
Prescott, Jr. At one point his mother separated the boys because
someone had told her it was good to give boys separate rooms. The
brothers did not like this and wanted to be in the same room
together. George Bush's boyhood nickname, in fact, was "Have
Half." He wanted to share things with others and take only half for
himself.

His deference to authority can also be understood in light of
the awesome parental models he had. Prescott Bush was an
imposing man who was six feet, four inches tall and had an
impressive career with the Harriman firm on Wall Street. At Yale,
he was a member of the Skull and Bones Society, Phi Beta Kappa,
and set a pattern that any young boy would find difficult to live up
to.

George Bush also had an impressive mother. Dorothy Bush provided a loving home with a lot of games, activities, discussions, and sports, but she was also very intrusive in some respects. For instance, she made George, a natural lefty, play tennis with his right hand. On one occasion, when he was angry because he had lost a tennis game, his mother said to him, "What game? You don't have any tennis game." She constantly told him to never brag about himself, always be humble, always write thank-you notes, and always be gracious.

Even as an adult on the campaign trail, he was subjected to her criticism that he engaged in too much braggadocio. When he was vice president, she once watched him read the text of one of Reagan's speeches as it was being delivered to a joint session of Congress. She asked him if he had read the speech. She thought it looked rude. "Why don't you just listen to him and hear it? You'll get it that way." Another time she told him, "Why don't you look at how Ronald Reagan treats Nancy. You never see him getting out of a plane first. He always is dealing with his wife by letting her go first and always being there." Thus, Bush received lessons from his mother throughout his life about not standing out in a way that suggested he was putting himself forward.

Throughout his life, conformity was rewarded with support and thus there was little need to rebel. His father got him his first job in Texas with a subsidiary of the Dresser Industries. When George Bush formed the Zapata Petroleum Corporation, his uncle provided a large percentage of the half-million dollars of capital that was required. When he went to the House of Representatives, his father was in the Senate and asked Arkansas Democrat Wilbur Mills to place him on the influential Ways and Means Committee. He was the first freshman in 60 years to have obtained a position of that sort. In his 1970 race for the Senate in Texas, he received $100,000 from the White House. Nixon, Agnew, and a host of other Republican heavies came and campaigned for him. When he lost that campaign, he was appointed U.N. ambassador, and the remainder of his career was through a series of appointments.

George Bush, in short, conformed and it paid off. He never really had to go out on his own and stand out by himself. Some indications suggest that this adaptation was not without physical costs. When Bush was in his early 30s, he had a bleeding ulcer. He said he learned through that experience to channel his anger into more direct channels. In May 1991 he had atrial fibrillation, and Graves' disease was diagnosed some time later. That disease, according to Dr. H. L. Abrams, a thyroid specialist at Stanford University, is often related to stress or results from a combination of bacteria and stress. Once a person has it, it creates even greater stress.

There are some indications that Bush was somewhat relieved that he had not won reelection as president. His first appearance after the election was before a small crowd at the Western Galleria Hotel in Houston. "The lines that for months had etched his face in worry, anger, and frustration," a *Los Angeles Times* reporter noted, "were less apparent than his pride in family, friends, and what he had accomplished." Bush seemed to prefer doing something noncontroversial. As he noted in his session with the press at the Western Galleria Hotel, "The nation should stand behind her new president." Bush personally pledged himself to take all of the steps necessary to ensure a smooth transition of power. Some staff aides later complained that Bush was overdoing it and that he was committing himself to the best transition ever. They were not happy about that situation. For most Americans, however, he showed the grace and skills that were his forte in those last official appearances.

QUESTION: Was there any basic weakness in Bush's campaign staff? Should it have included other individuals who knew what kind of man Bush was and who would have been able to push him forward?

MS. GLAD: His campaign staff tried. In the summer of 1992, political staff director Mary Matalin and other staff members were trying to get him on the campaign trail. He did not even want to have a meeting about the fall campaign, but they finally forced a meeting with him and decided on the running-on-the-record strategy. Mary Matalin wanted more but could not get more from him. He delayed going out on the campaign trail until the New Hampshire primary. Roger Ailes was obviously not with him. Ailes would have been able to run a thematic campaign that was much more effective. Bob Teeter had done some very good work for Bush during the primaries. He ran a good campaign for Ford in

1976. Bush's campaign staff were aware of the problems but simply could not get through to him.

QUESTION: You made no reference to Bush's military record. At a young age he became a fighter pilot, the youngest in the Navy. That record should subtract from the timid soul description of his personal character.

MS. GLAD: Yes, he won the Distinguished Flying Cross. In some respects, Bush is not a timid soul at all. He had a very distinguished and active career and was personally very courageous. I never understood the "wimp" attacks on him, frankly. I do not think he was a weak man, but he was a person who, in a sense, did not strike out on his own either intellectually or politically. Where the values are given and where action is clearly needed, George Bush can be very energetic and can excel.

When he attended Yale, he was Phi Beta Kappa and a member of Skull and Bones. He was a hard worker, especially in Texas. The fact that he received help does not detract from the feat of his building up his own offshore drilling company.

QUESTION: Did you ever meet Bush personally?

MS. GLAD: No, I haven't met him personally. Speechwriter Peggy Noonan noticed that he seemed to hate to use the word *I*. He says things like "Went fishing. Went out campaigning in the West." It is probably the result of his mother admonishing him not to talk about himself or be so egocentric. By not using the word *I*, he could get around that restriction.

John Podhoretz argues in his book, *Hell of a Ride: Backstage at the White House Follies, 1989–1993*, that sometimes when Bush did have a chance to talk about himself, he went on in great length. When he had the opportunity and felt it was proper, he could go into great detail about his accomplishments and avoid the use of the word *I* as much as possible.

QUESTION: Was James Baker unwilling or unable to get the campaign in shape when they brought him in at the last minute?

MS. GLAD: By the time Baker was asked to help, it was too late. He was brought in because they were getting desperate. The polls were showing that there were real problems. At the end, the polls were so bad that George Bush did not want to see them. His team quit their polling at the end of the campaign because it was discouraging them. Baker is someone Bush might have listened to earlier.

QUESTION: Do you think Bush was fatalistic from the beginning and thought that maybe he was not up to this campaign or another four years of the presidency?

MS. GLAD: At the beginning of his campaign, I think he thought he was going to win, and some complacency existed. Bush felt that his record was so good and that he had been such an excellent president that people would see it.

Bush was a person who not only did not like being a "good ol' boy" but who also did not like campaigning. He did not like the campaigning he did in 1988. He thought it was distasteful, and as a result, he put off campaigning for the 1992 election. When the reality of what was happening caught up to him, I think he became demoralized and did not respond effectively.

QUESTION: You indicated earlier that complete medical records for Mr. Bush are not yet available. Do you think there might have been some medical cause for the malaise of his reelection campaign? The characteristics you described were not so evident when he was elected the first time.

MS. GLAD: Dr. Abrams wrote a piece on this whole matter, and he indicated that in extreme cases—and this, he said, was not true of George Bush—what he calls a thyroid storm could occur in which the person can become very volatile and distracted and suffer from cognitive impairment during the hyperactive phase. Then when the thyroid is removed, the person can go flat and be depressed for a while, which can also impair cognitive functioning. Abrams says, however, that these judgments cannot be made without knowing the full record. I do think a possibility exists that Bush's passivity after the removal of his thyroid was partly medical.

QUESTION: Do you feel that his choice of Dan Quayle as his running mate could have added to Bush's failed reelection bid? Also, do you think that Bush chose a young man whom many people felt was not qualified to run because he felt insecure about choosing someone stronger for the vice-presidential spot?

MS. GLAD: Most of the studies that have been done on the importance of the vice president to a presidential candidacy suggest that it is not terribly crucial. Quayle was needed to buttress Bush's relationship to the Right in the party, so a political imperative was present that he had to follow. Maybe anxiety existed about Quayle because of Bush's health problems. I did receive several calls from the mass media after his atrial fibrillation in 1991, and also in January 1992 when he had his flu attack in Japan. The press did express concern. Whether the average person was concerned, I don't know.

Whether people are concerned about personal vulnerabilities or weaknesses depends on what the other candidate offers. There might have been some apprehension about Bush's health, but people were also apprehensive about Bill Clinton on the character issue. In some sense, one might even say that the two canceled each other out. People may have decided to stick with the issues in making their decisions due to apprehension about some of the personal qualities of each of the candidates.

QUESTION: How much of a role did Ross Perot's candidacy play in George Bush's defeat?

MS. GLAD: I think Ross Perot played a more crucial role in this campaign than can be documented at this point. Thirty-eight to 43 percent is not a huge margin by which to lose. Jimmy Carter got 42 percent of the vote in 1980, and Bill Clinton was only one percentage point ahead of Carter in the votes he received. Most of the exit polls show that Perot voters were almost evenly split between Bush and Clinton, although slightly more of them were Republicans. No one knows what people would do if they were really forced to choose. A strong independent party candidate in a race of that nature upsets everyone's calculations.

QUESTION: Do you think that a generation factor was important in the 1992 election? From my observation the Perot people tended to come from an older generation that would otherwise have voted for Bush. Do you have any documentation along those lines?

MS. GLAD: Yes, I do. Clinton got the youth vote, which had gone to Reagan earlier, so there was a real generational shift. His appearance on "The Arsenio Hall Show" with his sunglasses and playing the saxophone appealed to many young people.

Reagan's appeal to youth in 1980 and subsequently thereafter, as young people began moving in a more conservative direction, has sometimes been seen as a Republican realignment. However, Lance Bennett and others, including myself, see a political system in which people aren't aligned at all. They seem to be all over the place; the latest, most interesting story is what attracts them. Jay Rockefeller once said that people are against politicians and the media, but "the voters ain't so hot either." This disaffiliation from parties means that the voters are really not anchored, so it is a fight every day to keep plurality or approval ratings up or maintain the lead in the election.

QUESTION: If there had been some emphasis on the Republican side on welfare reform or if they had mentioned that what Clinton did was much like what the Republicans had done many years ago, would it have made a difference?

MS. GLAD: It might have made a difference if the Republicans had really pushed a substantive welfare reform program or if they had devised a moderate health insurance program. George Bush essentially ran on what he had done and not what he was going to do with the economy. The important thing is not that the economy was in such terrible shape, but that the indicators looked like it was getting worse. People were projecting into the future. The mass media, of course, was carrying all of the bad economic news, and that type of coverage obviously influences people a great deal.

It is hard to know where to place the mass media. Some of the conservative groups that follow the mass media point out the high number of negative stories about George Bush during the 1992 campaign, but Lance Bennett in his work observes that the top ten issues in 1992 included Gennifer Flowers, draft dodging, and other things that really hurt Bill Clinton. He therefore sees Bill Clinton as getting worse press. Both of them were getting bad press at various times.

QUESTION: Do you think rejection of gridlock and desire to have the same party in the White House and Congress had any real effect in the outcome?

MS. GLAD: It may have, but I have not seen any documentation to that effect.

NARRATOR: Several things of interest have arisen in the Bush oral history project. First, the Roger Mudd interview and others in the beginning seemed to portray a picture of someone who did not enjoy that kind of give-and-take, and it was a tough interview. Another factor is fatigue. Bush, like many former presidents, was tired, and that condition in itself could have contributed to his defeat. A similar point is that he did not show any enjoyment of the job during the campaign as he had in the beginning of his administration. Also, one or two of his intimates have said that Bush did not seem to want to talk about his job or issues with immediate colleagues. This view is countered by others who have a different view. Could any of these be used as factors in Bush's defeat?

MS. GLAD: They all could. Let's begin with the Dan Rather interview. That was not an impromptu interview. Cards were being put in front of Bush when he confronted Rather, so it was all planned in advance to show he was not a wimp. That interview laid to rest the wimp issue in the 1988 campaign, but CBS became the toughest on him during the subsequent part of the campaign season. The interview did not make him any friends at CBS.

In terms of fatigue, I'm sure he was tired. He was also very distressed at the charges being made during the campaign that he had been involved in the Iran-contra affair in insidious ways that had not yet been made public. The energy Bush showed at the beginning of his term was in large part demonstrated by showing people around the White House, entertaining the reporters at horseshoes, boat riding, and other similar activities. Yet from the beginning, people were saying he was slow in assessing what his policy toward the Soviet Union should be and in making personnel decisions. Many of the things that are being said about Clinton were said about Bush early in 1989. Lesley Stahl, among others, said that fairly early about Bush. Bush also had a fairly short honeymoon, so fatigue and sensitivity to criticism certainly affected him.

NARRATOR: Some of Bush's staff people felt that in the beginning of the administration, Bush enjoyed the exchange of ideas on questions of policy and the direction in which the country was going. Later, however, he really wasn't anxious to respond when these people engaged him, and he did not show enjoyment for the job. Could you comment on this difference in Bush's attitude?

MS. GLAD: Bush was a person who had been used to doing his best and being rewarded for his efforts. The presidency is a different kind of situation. In the presidency today, the president is subject to an onslaught that many people would find difficult. George Bush was a person who was used to being a good guy and getting approval for it, and he was not quite prepared for the heat he would take. Many of the top people today are not running for president because of what they are put through. The media holds up standards that are truly extraordinary. When Bush settled for a modest tax increase to try to cut the deficit in 1990 and get something out of the Democratic Congress, the reaction from the media was, "Why have you gone against your promise?" Instead of saying, "OK, good boy, now you see reality," they were saying that anyone who does not do what he promised in the campaign should be subjected to 20 lashes. The media holds up standards that make it extremely difficult for any politician to operate.

NARRATOR: Does any evidence exist to the contrary on this "good ol' boy" issue? It could not have been pleasant for George Bush to send people to their death, yet he never hesitated with regard to Panama, which was a bloody campaign for those who were there. He certainly never hesitated in making decisions about the Persian Gulf War. He acted with great energy and detachment, not ever being sure whether his decision would result in a victory or a defeat. Is there any contrary evidence that shows he was a courageous president and set aside his notions of personal esteem when he had to make decisions of that kind?

MS. GLAD: George Bush did have a courageous side, provided it was something he knew was the right thing to do in terms of his upbringing, the values he had, and what the people around him thought he should do. In terms of the war against Iraq, Secretary of Defense Dick Cheney and National Security Adviser Brent Scowcroft favored going ahead. His closest intimates were with him on that issue.

It is true that Senator Sam Nunn, the head of the CIA, and others were raising questions about how risky it might be. I do not think anyone has the full story. The real issue is whether Bush thought it was risky or not. Certainly to many on the outside, it did not look like a foregone conclusion that the victory would be so easy. It might have resulted in many American deaths and really hurt him politically, whether he knew it or not.

In view of what happened, Bush got 89 to 90 percent in the popularity ratings at the polls. When he did not go after Saddam Hussein and the United States did not finish Saddam off, however, the polls showed that people were no longer saying that he did a great job with Iraq because the United States did not finish the job. Anyone who is concerned with balance-of-power politics would say that Bush could not finish the job because seriously weakening Iraq would leave Iran as the major force in the area. It was sensible that he stopped when he did. Again, however, many in the media and the American public prefer black-and-white answers, and Bush suffered as a consequence.

QUESTION: Do you think Mr. Bush felt obligated to run for a second term, although he did not want to?

MS. GLAD: Bush really thought he would win a second term and that his record would speak for itself. It was only when he got further into the campaign that he discovered he was in trouble. I think he did not see his campaign as being in great difficulty until the fall of 1992.

QUESTION: After being in or near the Oval Office, was there a possibility of occupational fatigue? Bush might have thought he would win and that it was his duty to seek another term. If he had had free choice, he may not have wanted to go further.

MS. GLAD: Rather than saying either/or, one could say that he was ambivalent about it because he had been subject to an increasing amount of criticism. Being in that situation isn't pleasant for anyone. The fact that he appeared to be relieved when he lost the election and the campaign was over indicates that a side of him may not have wanted to run. I think, however, there was a side of him that did want to run. Human beings can be very ambivalent. Afterward, of course, he was depressed. He was hurt by the rejection of the American people whom he felt he had done his best to serve. It may not be that he was turned out of the job so much as he did not receive the kind of approval, understanding, or recognition of his work that he felt he deserved.

NARRATOR: Does any information support the lonely president idea with regard to Bush? Part of his own party did not think he was a Republican and was not particularly supportive of him. Democrats were not supportive. Do you agree with the argument that Bush stood alone on some domestic issues more than some presidents have and that he needed Sununu because the Right was hostile, despite the convention and other things?

MS. GLAD: I agree with what you are saying. In some respects Bush's position was lonely. He acted responsibly in 1990 on the budget, but many House Republicans signed a manifest blasting him for his betrayal of his campaign promises. What was a statesman-like act was seen as a betrayal by others. Then Patrick Buchanan said that he was worse than Ted Kennedy and had betrayed the people. That criticism was pretty hard to take.

NARRATOR: Professor Betty Glad has become one of the standard bearers of Miller Center Forums, and we thank her very much for her discussion of the Bush presidential election.